Justice in the Ashes

Echoes of War: The Russia-Ukraine Conflict and Its Global Ripples, Volume 6

SANDEEP CHAVAN

Published by SANDEEP CHAVAN, 2024.

JUSTICE IN THE ASHES

First edition. December 20, 2024.

ISBN: 979-8230550679

Written by SANDEEP CHAVAN.

Table of Contents

This book is dedicated to the victims of war crimes, atrocities, and human rights violations worldwide. It is also a tribute to the advocates for justice—investigators, journalists, civil society organizations, and legal practitioners—who relentlessly strive to ensure that no atrocity goes unpunished and no voice is silenced.

May this book serve as a testament to humanity's enduring commitment to fairness, accountability, and the dignity of life. Let it inspire future generations to pursue justice without borders, fostering a more equitable and peaceful world.

"To those who suffered in silence and to those who spoke for them: May justice prevail."

"In the ashes of conflict, justice is the first seed of hope."— Anonymous

Disclaimer

The content of this book, *Justice in the Ashes: Accountability in the Russia-Ukraine War*, is intended for informational and educational purposes only. While every effort has been made to ensure the accuracy and relevance of the information presented, the author and publisher make no representations or warranties regarding the completeness, timeliness, or applicability of the content. The views expressed in this book are those of the author and do not necessarily reflect the opinions of any specific institution, organization, or entity.

This book includes analysis and commentary on historical and contemporary events, supported by publicly available data and research. It is not intended as legal, political, or professional advice. Readers are encouraged to consult appropriate experts or sources for advice tailored to their specific needs or circumstances.

References to institutions, organizations, or individuals are based on publicly available information and are used solely for illustrative or contextual purposes. No endorsement or affiliation is implied. Similarly, any errors or omissions are unintentional and will be corrected in subsequent editions, where possible.

The author and publisher disclaim any liability for any actions taken or not taken based on the content of this book. The use of this book is at the reader's own risk, and the author and publisher shall not be held responsible for any consequences resulting from its use.

This book addresses sensitive topics, including war crimes, human rights violations, and global justice. Readers should approach the material with discretion and an understanding of its potentially emotional impact. Any parallels drawn between events, systems, or individuals are intended to promote understanding and dialogue, not to assign blame or judgment.

By engaging with this book, readers acknowledge and accept the limitations inherent in its scope and purpose.

Preface

The concept of justice is as old as human civilization, yet it remains one of the most challenging pursuits in our modern world. In the shadow of devastating conflicts, the demand for accountability often confronts the harsh realities of geopolitics, societal divisions, and the limitations of global institutions. This book, *Justice in the Ashes: Accountability in the Russia-Ukraine War,* seeks to navigate this complex terrain, offering an exploration of how justice can be pursued amidst the chaos of war and the shifting dynamics of power.

The Russia-Ukraine conflict has not only reshaped the geopolitical landscape but also served as a stark reminder of the fragility of international law. As war crimes and atrocities unfolded, the global community found itself grappling with how to document, address, and prosecute these acts in real-time. This conflict, like many before it, underscores the pressing need for robust mechanisms that ensure justice is served, even amidst the most trying circumstances.

This book is not merely an account of the events in Russia and Ukraine; it is an inquiry into the broader themes of international justice. It examines the systems designed to uphold accountability, their triumphs, and their failures. It delves into the evolution of global legal frameworks, the transformative role of technology, and the critical importance of civil society in bridging gaps where institutions falter. Above all, it emphasizes the voices of victims and survivors—those for whom justice is not an abstract concept but a tangible necessity.

The journey of writing this book has been one of reflection and discovery. Drawing from historical precedents like the Nuremberg Trials, the ICTY, and the ICTR, this work places the Russia-Ukraine war within a continuum of efforts to combat impunity and uphold human dignity. At the same time, it confronts the unique challenges of our time—challenges defined by technological advancements, non-state actors, and an increasingly polarized world.

This book is dedicated to the victims of war crimes and their advocates, whose courage and resilience continue to inspire the pursuit of justice. It is my hope that this work not only informs but also challenges readers to think critically about the systems we have in place and the reforms we must undertake.

As you journey through the pages of this book, may you be reminded of the enduring power of accountability to rebuild trust, heal societies, and create a foundation for peace. Justice, as I have come to understand it, is not merely a destination but an ongoing process—one that demands our collective commitment to fairness, truth, and humanity.

Sandeep Chavan

Author

Introduction: Justice in the Midst of Chaos

The echoes of war reverberate far beyond the battlefield, leaving scars on humanity that can last generations. The Russia-Ukraine war is no exception. This conflict, while geographically concentrated, has captured global attention due to its implications on human rights, international law, and the fragile fabric of global order. Amid the chaos of artillery fire, displaced families, and political posturing, a profound question emerges: How does one ensure justice when the perpetrators are shielded by the very systems meant to hold them accountable?

At its core, the pursuit of justice in war transcends individual conflicts; it is a collective assertion that humanity will not tolerate atrocities, no matter the perpetrator. This pursuit is not merely a legal exercise but a moral imperative that resonates deeply with the global community. The Russia-Ukraine war, with its harrowing tales of bombed-out cities, civilian massacres, and forced displacements, demands accountability not just to honor its victims but to deter future acts of inhumanity.

Framing the Russia-Ukraine War within the Context of Accountability

The Russia-Ukraine war, the first major interstate conflict in Europe since the Balkan wars of the 1990s, has jolted the world into revisiting the concept of accountability in modern warfare. Unlike internal conflicts or insurgencies, interstate wars often have broader implications, affecting international stability and global norms. This conflict, with its profound human cost and geopolitical repercussions, has spotlighted the fragile systems designed to address war crimes and hold perpetrators accountable. The question is not just about documenting crimes but about the global community's willingness and ability to act on them.

Historical Foundations and the Imperfect Mechanisms of Justice

The foundations for modern accountability in war crimes were laid in the aftermath of World War II, with the Nuremberg Trials marking a watershed moment in international law. These trials set precedents for holding individuals—not just states—responsible for atrocities, emphasizing that "following orders" is not a defense against crimes against humanity. Yet, despite these achievements, the mechanisms for justice remain far from perfect.

The creation of institutions like the International Criminal Court (ICC) aimed to address these gaps, but their effectiveness has been inconsistent. The ICC, for instance, relies on state cooperation to apprehend suspects and conduct trials—a challenging proposition when dealing with powerful nations. Furthermore, its jurisdiction is limited by geopolitics, as countries like Russia have not ratified the Rome Statute that established the ICC. This lack of universal jurisdiction creates significant hurdles in ensuring accountability, particularly in conflicts involving states outside the ICC's reach.

The Challenges of Accountability Amid Ongoing Hostilities

In the Russia-Ukraine war, the pursuit of justice faces additional complexities due to the ongoing nature of the conflict. Unlike post-conflict tribunals, where evidence is gathered after hostilities have ceased, the Russia-Ukraine war presents a live and volatile situation. Investigators face immense challenges in accessing war zones, verifying reports, and ensuring the security of witnesses and evidence.

The stories emerging from the conflict are deeply troubling. Reports of civilian massacres, the deliberate targeting of hospitals, schools, and other civilian infrastructure, and the alleged use of cluster munitions and other banned weapons highlight a disturbing pattern of behavior. These are not isolated incidents but indications of systemic violations that demand urgent investigation. However, in the heat of war, gathering credible evidence and ensuring impartiality is fraught with difficulties.

Geopolitical Realities and the Limits of Justice

Adding to these challenges is the fact that one of the key actors in the conflict, Russia, holds a permanent seat on the United Nations Security Council (UNSC). This position grants it significant power, including the ability to veto resolutions that could lead to investigations or sanctions. This dynamic exemplifies the inherent contradictions in the global justice system, where the same nations tasked with upholding international law can obstruct its enforcement.

The war has exposed uncomfortable truths about the selective application of justice in international affairs. Historically, accountability has often been shaped by the balance of power rather than the rule of law. While weaker nations or individuals without state protection have faced prosecution, powerful states and their leaders have often evaded accountability due to their geopolitical influence.

The Russia-Ukraine war forces the world to confront these contradictions. It highlights the urgent need to reform international institutions to ensure they can function impartially, regardless of the power dynamics involved. At the same time, it underscores the importance of preserving the credibility of international law, as selective enforcement risks undermining the entire system.

The Broader Implications for Global Justice

The implications of the Russia-Ukraine war extend far beyond the immediate conflict zone. If the global community fails to hold perpetrators accountable, it risks normalizing impunity for war crimes. This would embolden aggressors in other regions, undermining international norms and increasing the likelihood of future atrocities. On the other hand, a robust and impartial pursuit of justice could serve as a deterrent, reinforcing the principle that no one is above the law.

In this context, the Russia-Ukraine war serves as both a challenge and an opportunity for the global justice system. It challenges the existing mechanisms by exposing their weaknesses but also offers an opportunity to strengthen and adapt them for the complexities of modern warfare. The question is whether the world will rise to this occasion or allow politics and power to overshadow the pursuit of justice.

In conclusion, framing the Russia-Ukraine war within the context of accountability reveals a complex and multifaceted struggle. It is a test of the global community's resolve to uphold the principles of justice and the rule of law. Amid the devastation and suffering, the pursuit of accountability stands as a beacon of hope—not just for the victims of this war but for humanity as a whole. The lessons learned here will shape the future of international justice and determine whether it can rise above political constraints to truly serve the cause of humanity.

Why War Crimes Matter to the Global Community

War crimes represent the darkest chapters in human history. These acts, from genocide to the deliberate targeting of civilians, are not merely violations of international law—they are assaults on the fundamental principles that bind humanity together. They challenge the essence of what it means to be civilized, forcing the world to confront the depths of human cruelty. The devastation caused by such crimes reverberates far beyond the immediate victims, leaving scars on communities, nations, and the collective conscience of humanity.

The Universal Importance of Accountability

Ensuring accountability for war crimes transcends individual conflicts and national borders. It is a global endeavor to affirm that certain lines cannot be crossed without consequences. War crimes are not merely domestic issues; they are affronts to universal values—human dignity, the sanctity of life, and the rule of law. When the global community fails to address these atrocities, it risks eroding these shared principles, allowing chaos to replace order and undermining the progress made in establishing a just world.

Justice for war crimes is not solely about punishing the perpetrators. It is also about restoring dignity to the victims, acknowledging their suffering, and creating a record of truth that can serve as a foundation for healing and reconciliation. Without this accountability, survivors are left to grapple with the injustice of their experiences, and societies remain haunted by unresolved traumas.

The Russia-Ukraine War: A Global Test of Principles

The Russia-Ukraine war has placed the global community at a critical crossroads. This conflict is not just a localized dispute; it is a test of resilience, principles, and the effectiveness of international law. Reports of deliberate attacks on civilian infrastructure, forced displacements, and other atrocities have shocked the world, demanding a decisive response. Yet, addressing these crimes is not straightforward. Political considerations often complicate justice, as nations weigh their strategic interests against moral imperatives.

The international response to the Russia-Ukraine war will set a precedent for how the world addresses future conflicts. If accountability is pursued with determination, it can reinforce the principle that no one is above the law, regardless of their power or position. However, if political calculations overshadow justice, the message sent to aggressors worldwide will be one of impunity—a green light for further violations.

The Dangerous Precedent of Impunity

The denial of justice in cases of war crimes has far-reaching consequences. When perpetrators go unpunished, it signals to others that they too can act with impunity. This not only emboldens aggressors but also undermines the credibility of international institutions designed to uphold justice. Over time, the erosion of these mechanisms can lead to a more chaotic and unstable world, where might makes right, and the rule of law is replaced by the rule of power.

The consequences of inaction extend beyond the immediate conflict. Impunity can destabilize entire regions, create cycles of violence, and foster resentment that fuels extremism and terrorism. It can also weaken the trust of smaller nations in the international system, as they see that justice is selectively applied and often inaccessible to the most vulnerable.

Accountability as a Deterrent

On the other hand, pursuing justice for war crimes can serve as a powerful deterrent. It sends a clear message that violations of international law will not be tolerated and that perpetrators, regardless of their status, will be held accountable. This not only helps prevent future atrocities but also reinforces the idea that global norms and laws are more than mere words—they are binding principles that govern the conduct of nations and individuals alike.

Justice also plays a crucial role in reconciliation and rebuilding after conflict. By addressing past wrongs and ensuring accountability, societies can begin to heal and move forward. The acknowledgment of crimes and the punishment of those responsible can help bridge divides, foster trust, and lay the groundwork for lasting peace.

In conclusion, the Russia-Ukraine war is more than a geopolitical struggle; it is a moral challenge for the global community. War crimes matter not only because they violate the law but because they undermine the very foundation of a just and humane world. How the world responds to these crimes will shape the trajectory of international relations and determine whether future conflicts can be managed within the bounds of law and humanity. If justice prevails, it will reaffirm the global commitment to the sanctity of human life and the rule of law. If it fails, it will set a dangerous precedent, leaving the door open for greater atrocities and a more fractured world. The stakes could not be higher, and the time for decisive action is now.

The Delicate Balance between Politics and Justice

Justice in the context of war is rarely a straightforward endeavor. It operates in a murky space where law and politics intersect, often clashing in ways that dilute even the noblest of intentions. While the principles of justice are universal, their application is frequently influenced by geopolitical considerations, strategic alliances, and the competing interests of powerful nations. In such a landscape, ensuring accountability for war crimes becomes a challenging, often contentious task.

The Intricacies of Accountability in War

Holding individuals or states accountable for war crimes requires more than just evidence and legal frameworks. It demands a delicate balance between moral imperatives and political realities. Evidence must be meticulously documented, legal cases must be constructed, and international mechanisms must be engaged—all while navigating the reluctance or outright resistance of states that may have vested interests in the conflict.

In the case of the Russia-Ukraine war, this balancing act is particularly precarious. The conflict involves not just two nations but a web of alliances and rivalries that complicate efforts to uphold justice. Countries supporting Ukraine, such as the United States and European nations, have their own geopolitical stakes, while Russia's position as a global power adds another layer of complexity. This dynamic has led to accusations of selective accountability, where justice is pursued against one side while ignoring violations by the other.

The Role of International Institutions

International institutions like the International Criminal Court (ICC) are designed to function as impartial arbiters of justice, yet their role in conflicts like the Russia-Ukraine war is fraught with challenges. The ICC's mandate is clear: to investigate and prosecute individuals responsible for war crimes, crimes against humanity, and genocide. However, the institution's effectiveness is often undermined by practical and political constraints.

One significant limitation is the ICC's reliance on state cooperation. Without the ability to enforce its rulings independently, the court must depend on member states to arrest suspects and execute decisions. In conflicts involving powerful nations, such as Russia, this reliance often renders the ICC powerless, as those nations may refuse to recognize its jurisdiction or comply with its rulings.

Moreover, the ICC has faced accusations of bias and selective prosecution, particularly in cases where political considerations appear to influence its actions. Critics argue that the court disproportionately targets leaders from weaker nations while avoiding cases involving major powers or their allies. For victims and survivors, these shortcomings are not just procedural failures—they are profound betrayals of their suffering and a blow to the credibility of international justice.

The Russia-Ukraine War: A Test Case for Global Justice

The ongoing Russia-Ukraine war serves as a stark reminder of the challenges inherent in pursuing justice during active conflict. Documenting atrocities and identifying perpetrators is difficult enough in the chaos of war, but achieving accountability in this case is further complicated by the geopolitical stakes. Russia's position as a permanent member of the United Nations Security Council (UNSC) allows it to wield veto power over resolutions that might hold it accountable, effectively shielding itself from meaningful international action.

This dynamic has exposed the fragility of global justice mechanisms and the extent to which they are shaped by power dynamics. It raises uncomfortable questions about the ability of international law to function impartially in the face of such constraints. As a result, the pursuit of justice in the Russia-Ukraine war is as much about addressing the immediate consequences of the conflict as it is about confronting the broader structural weaknesses of the international system.

The Broader Stakes for Humanity

The stakes in this conflict extend far beyond the region. Ensuring justice amid the chaos is about more than punishing the guilty or addressing the needs of victims; it is about safeguarding the principles of humanity for generations to come. Failure to hold perpetrators accountable risks normalizing impunity for war crimes, setting a dangerous precedent for future conflicts.

Moreover, the lack of accountability undermines trust in international institutions, weakening their ability to respond to crises and protect vulnerable populations. For victims, it signals that their suffering is secondary to geopolitical considerations—a devastating blow to their hope for justice and closure.

Navigating Political Pressures and Legal Constraints

The challenge of pursuing justice lies not only in documenting atrocities and building legal cases but also in navigating the intricate web of political pressures that accompany such efforts. Nations involved in the conflict, either directly or indirectly, often prioritize their strategic interests over moral considerations. This creates a complex and often contradictory environment where the pursuit of justice is hindered by the very actors who claim to champion it.

Despite these challenges, the pursuit of justice in the Russia-Ukraine war remains a moral and legal necessity. It is a test of the global community's resolve to uphold the principles of humanity and ensure that even in the midst of chaos, accountability prevails.

In conclusion, the delicate balance between politics and justice is a defining feature of accountability in the context of war. While international law provides the framework for addressing war crimes, its implementation is often constrained by the realities of global power dynamics. The Russia-Ukraine war highlights these tensions, offering both a challenge and an opportunity for the international community. By navigating these complexities with determination and integrity, the world can reaffirm its commitment to justice and demonstrate that even in the darkest times, the principles of humanity endure.

Conclusion

In the ashes of war, amidst the shattered homes and broken lives, the pursuit of justice emerges as a beacon of hope. It is a testament to humanity's enduring commitment to fairness, accountability, and the belief that even in the darkest of times, principles of decency and morality can prevail. The devastation wrought by the Russia-Ukraine war is a stark reminder of the cost of conflict, yet it also provides an unparalleled opportunity for the global community to reaffirm its shared values and aspirations for a just world.

Justice in the context of war is not merely about punishing perpetrators; it is about restoring humanity's faith in its collective ability to rise above the chaos. It is about giving voice to the voiceless, ensuring that the pain and suffering of victims are neither ignored nor forgotten. Justice, in its truest form, is the acknowledgment that the dignity of human life transcends borders, politics, and power.

The Russia-Ukraine war presents a unique challenge—a litmus test for the effectiveness of international justice mechanisms in an era marked by geopolitical complexity. It also serves as a call to action for nations, institutions, and individuals to work collectively in confronting the atrocities of war. As this conflict unfolds, the global community stands at a crossroads, where inaction could set dangerous precedents, but decisive efforts could fortify the foundations of international law and human rights.

This book delves into this intricate and often fraught journey of seeking justice amid conflict. Through its pages, we will explore not only the legal frameworks and political dynamics that shape accountability but also the stories of resilience, courage, and determination from individuals and organizations dedicated to this cause. We will examine the triumphs that inspire hope, the failures that expose systemic weaknesses, and the lessons that can guide the world toward a more just and humane future.

The pursuit of justice in the Russia-Ukraine war is not just a task for lawyers, diplomats, or activists—it is a shared responsibility of humanity. It is a reminder that while war may bring destruction, justice can lay the groundwork for peace, healing, and reconciliation. In doing so, it reaffirms the belief that even in the face of unimaginable suffering, the ideals of fairness and accountability are not mere abstractions but tangible forces capable of transforming despair into hope.

As we embark on this exploration, let us carry forward the conviction that justice, though challenging and often imperfect, remains an indispensable cornerstone of a civilized world. Let this journey inspire us to believe that in the relentless pursuit of accountability, humanity can indeed rise above the ashes of war and chart a path toward a future defined by compassion, respect, and enduring peace.

1. Tracing the Origins of War Crimes

The concept of war crimes, as we understand it today, represents humanity's collective attempt to impose moral and legal boundaries on the chaos of warfare. While war has often been seen as an inevitable aspect of human history, the idea that certain acts during conflict are universally unacceptable reflects a significant evolution in societal values. From the earliest codes of conduct to the detailed frameworks of modern international law, the origins of war crimes trace a journey where ethics and justice have sought to tame the brutality of war. This chapter delves into the roots of these principles, exploring how ancient traditions, historical milestones, and pivotal events have shaped the laws that define and prosecute war crimes in the present day.

1.1 Defining War Crimes: Acts That Cross the Line

War crimes represent the gravest violations of the laws of war, starkly reminding us that even in the chaos of conflict, certain actions are universally unacceptable. Defined under international law, these acts breach rules established by treaties such as the Geneva Conventions and customary international humanitarian law. They include willful killing, torture, taking hostages, targeting civilians, and the use of prohibited weapons. What distinguishes war crimes from other violations is their severity and direct affront to the fundamental principles of humanity.

What Constitutes a War Crime Under International Law?

A war crime occurs when individuals—be they soldiers, commanders, or political leaders—violate established rules of war, resulting in harm to those not actively participating in hostilities. The Geneva Conventions, widely regarded as the foundation of modern humanitarian law, provide specific protections for civilians, medical personnel, prisoners of war, and cultural heritage. Acts such as intentionally targeting hospitals, starving civilian populations, or deploying chemical or biological weapons constitute clear breaches of these principles.

The Rome Statute of the International Criminal Court (ICC) further codifies war crimes, offering a detailed list of offenses under its jurisdiction. Crucially, these crimes must occur during an armed conflict, and establishing culpability requires demonstrating the perpetrator's intent to carry out such acts. This emphasis on intentionality underscores the gravity of these offenses in the context of armed conflict.

Distinguishing War Crimes from Crimes Against Humanity and Genocide

While war crimes are defined by their connection to breaches of the rules of war, they differ from crimes against humanity and genocide in both scope and context:

- **Crimes against humanity** involve widespread or systematic attacks against civilian populations, such as enslavement, deportation, or persecution. These acts can occur in times of peace or war and are not necessarily tied to battlefield dynamics.
- **Genocide**, however, is marked by the intent to destroy, in whole or in part, a national, ethnic, racial, or religious group. Its defining feature is the deliberate eradication of a group's identity and existence, often carried out with precision and calculated intent.

Understanding these distinctions is essential in international law, as each category carries unique implications for prosecution, jurisdiction, and global response. While some overlap exists, war crimes are explicitly rooted in the violation of laws governing armed conflict.

Why Certain Acts Are Universally Condemned

The universal condemnation of war crimes stems from their devastating impact on human dignity and the social fabric of communities. Deliberate acts such as targeting civilians, employing banned weapons, or destroying cultural heritage transcend individual harm, striking at the core values that underpin civilization. These actions disregard fundamental humanitarian principles of proportionality, distinction, and necessity, which aim to minimize suffering during war.

For instance, the deliberate targeting of schools and hospitals not only causes immediate loss of life but also cripples a community's future by depriving it of education and healthcare. Similarly, the use of banned weapons, such as cluster munitions or chemical agents, leaves long-term scars on both people and the environment, affecting generations to come.

By categorizing these acts as war crimes, the international community reinforces the principle that even war must have boundaries. Those who breach these boundaries must be held accountable. This framework not only serves as a deterrent but also provides a foundation for justice, ensuring that perpetrators cannot act with impunity. As the world grapples with ongoing conflicts, such as the Russia-Ukraine war, the importance of these definitions remains critical in guiding efforts to document, prosecute, and ultimately prevent such atrocities.

1.2 The Genesis of Accountability: From Ancient Codes to Modern Laws

The pursuit of justice in warfare is deeply rooted in history, reflecting humanity's ongoing effort to balance power with morality and impose order on the chaos of conflict. From early legal codes to the sophisticated frameworks of modern international law, the journey toward holding individuals and nations accountable reveals an enduring struggle to define and uphold ethical conduct in war.

Early Attempts at Regulating Warfare

The origins of wartime accountability can be traced to ancient legal codes and traditions that sought to mitigate violence. The **Code of Hammurabi**, one of the earliest known legal documents from ancient Mesopotamia, outlined rudimentary rules for conduct in conflict, emphasizing proportional retribution and the protection of certain groups. While primarily domestic in scope, its principles hinted at a broader aspiration to restrain excessive violence.

In ancient India, the **Laws of Manu** provided ethical guidelines for warfare, stressing the protection of civilians and prohibiting certain weapons. Similarly, **Sun Tzu's Art of War** in China offered strategic advice that incorporated elements of restraint and moral consideration, recognizing the destructive potential of unchecked violence.

The **laws of chivalry**, which emerged in medieval Europe, introduced a moral dimension to the conduct of knights and soldiers. While often romanticized, these codes emphasized the protection of non-combatants, humane treatment of prisoners, and the avoidance of unnecessary destruction. Rooted in feudal and religious structures, these traditions laid important groundwork for later efforts to codify the rules of war.

The Influence of Philosophy, Religion, and Cultural Norms

Philosophy, religion, and cultural norms have profoundly shaped humanity's understanding of justice in warfare. Ancient Greek philosophers like **Socrates** and **Aristotle** debated the ethics of war, advocating principles that balanced necessity with compassion. The concept of a **"just war"**, later elaborated by Roman thinkers like **Cicero**, emphasized that wars should be waged only for legitimate reasons and conducted with restraint.

Religious teachings also contributed significantly to wartime ethics. The **Ten Commandments** in Judeo-Christian traditions, Islamic teachings on **jihad**, and Buddhism's emphasis on **non-violence** all shaped societal norms that discouraged unnecessary brutality. Though interpreted differently across cultures, these principles formed a moral foundation for limiting harm during conflict.

Cultural practices among indigenous tribes in Africa, the Americas, and Oceania also played a role. These communities often developed rituals and agreements governing warfare, emphasizing reconciliation and minimizing harm to vulnerable groups. Such practices, though informal, reflected a shared understanding of the need to preserve human dignity even in times of strife.

The Transition to Codified International Law

The 19th and early 20th centuries marked a transformative era in the regulation of warfare, as moral and ethical considerations evolved into formalized international laws. The **Lieber Code of 1863**, developed during the American Civil War, was a pioneering effort to codify military conduct. It emphasized the protection of civilians, humane treatment of prisoners, and the prohibition of unnecessary destruction. This code influenced subsequent international agreements, such as the **Hague Conventions** of 1899 and 1907, which established comprehensive rules for land and naval warfare.

The **Geneva Conventions**, first adopted in 1864 and later expanded, provided a universal framework for protecting the wounded, prisoners of war, and civilians. These conventions remain central to modern international humanitarian law, reflecting humanity's collective aspiration to limit suffering in armed conflict.

The early 20th century also saw the establishment of international institutions like the **League of Nations** and later the **United Nations**, which sought to prevent conflicts and hold violators accountable. The post-World War II **Nuremberg Trials** marked a watershed moment in accountability, setting enduring precedents for prosecuting war crimes and crimes against humanity.

Thus, the genesis of accountability in warfare illustrates a gradual but determined effort to impose moral and legal order on the brutality of conflict. From ancient legal codes and philosophical principles to the development of modern international law, each step reflects humanity's evolving recognition of the need for justice. These historical milestones not only provide valuable context for understanding war crimes but also offer a foundation for addressing the complex challenges of accountability in contemporary conflicts, such as the Russia-Ukraine war.

1.3 The Nuremberg Trials: A Turning Point for Justice

The Nuremberg Trials represent a landmark in the history of international law, marking the first time the global community formally acknowledged that individuals—not just states—must be held accountable for crimes committed during war. In the aftermath of the unprecedented atrocities of World War II, these trials laid the foundation for modern concepts of war crimes, crimes against humanity, and mechanisms of accountability. Their influence continues to shape the pursuit of justice in contemporary conflicts.

Shaping Modern Concepts of War Crimes and Accountability

World War II exposed the depths of human cruelty, leaving the global community grappling with the scale of suffering inflicted by Nazi Germany and its allies. The systematic extermination of millions during the Holocaust, the deliberate targeting of civilian populations, and the exploitation of forced labor camps shocked the conscience of humanity. These atrocities underscored the need for a legal framework to ensure that such acts would not go unpunished.

The Nuremberg Trials, held from 1945 to 1946, were convened to address this unprecedented wrongdoing. For the first time, an international tribunal held individuals accountable for actions that violated the moral and legal principles underpinning civilized society. Heads of state, military commanders, and other officials were prosecuted, dismantling the notion that national sovereignty or following orders could shield perpetrators from justice.

Central to the trials was the introduction of new legal concepts, including **crimes against humanity**, which addressed atrocities such as mass murder, enslavement, and systematic persecution of civilian populations. These trials reinforced the principle that individuals have a duty to uphold international law, even when acting under national directives.

Key Precedents Set by the Nuremberg Trials

The Nuremberg Trials established critical precedents that continue to guide international law:

Individual Responsibility: The trials affirmed that individuals, regardless of their rank or position, could be held personally accountable for war crimes. This shattered the defense of "state sovereignty" as a shield against prosecution.

Crimes Against Humanity: The concept of crimes against humanity was formally codified, addressing violations that transcended the laws of war and constituted affronts to human dignity on a global scale. This provided a legal basis for prosecuting acts such as genocide and systemic persecution.

Rejection of the "Following Orders" Defense: The trials rejected the defense that individuals were simply following orders, establishing the expectation that moral judgment must guide actions, even in hierarchical systems. This principle remains a cornerstone of international justice.

Legal Framework for International Justice: The Nuremberg Trials laid the groundwork for subsequent developments in international law, including the expansion of the Geneva Conventions and the establishment of the International Criminal Court (ICC).

Lessons Learned and Their Impact on Subsequent Conflicts

The legacy of the Nuremberg Trials extends far beyond the prosecution of Nazi war criminals. They provided a blueprint for addressing accountability in later conflicts, offering both legal and moral guidance for future tribunals. The principles established at Nuremberg were echoed in the **Tokyo Trials**, which prosecuted Japanese leaders for similar atrocities after World War II.

In subsequent decades, the lessons of Nuremberg informed the creation of ad hoc tribunals for conflicts in the former Yugoslavia and Rwanda. These tribunals sought to address ethnic cleansing, genocide, and other atrocities, drawing directly on the precedents of individual responsibility and crimes against humanity established at Nuremberg.

However, the trials also revealed enduring challenges. They faced criticism for their "victor's justice" approach, as only Axis powers were prosecuted, while crimes committed by the Allies were largely overlooked. This highlighted the tension between the ideals of justice and the geopolitical realities of international relations—a challenge that remains relevant in conflicts like the Russia-Ukraine war.

In short, the Nuremberg Trials were a watershed moment in the evolution of international law, demonstrating the global community's commitment to ensuring that war crimes and atrocities do not go unpunished. They set powerful precedents for individual accountability, established the legal foundation for prosecuting crimes against humanity, and underscored the importance of upholding moral and legal standards during conflict.

As the world continues to confront modern conflicts, the lessons of Nuremberg remain profoundly relevant. They remind us that justice, though often constrained by politics and imperfect in its execution, is a vital force in upholding humanity's principles. The trials serve as both a historical milestone and a guide for addressing the challenges of accountability in today's turbulent world.

1.4 The Geneva Conventions: Establishing Rules for Humanity in War

The Geneva Conventions are the bedrock of modern international humanitarian law, embodying humanity's enduring effort to impose order and ethical conduct amid the chaos of war. Adopted in response to the brutal realities of 19th and early 20th-century conflicts, these treaties establish clear rules to protect those who do not participate in hostilities, including civilians, prisoners of war, and medical personnel. By codifying humane conduct and defining war crimes, the Geneva Conventions have become the global benchmark for assessing wartime accountability.

An Overview of the Geneva Conventions

The Geneva Conventions comprise four core treaties and three additional protocols, first adopted in 1864 and significantly expanded in 1949. They arose from the efforts of the **International Committee of the Red Cross (ICRC)**, spearheaded by Henri Dunant, who sought to alleviate the suffering of soldiers wounded during the Battle of Solferino. Over time, these treaties evolved to address the complexities of modern warfare and ensure the protection of vulnerable groups.

The 1949 Geneva Conventions, ratified by nearly every nation, outline protections for:

- **Wounded and sick soldiers on land during war** (*First Convention*).
- **Wounded, sick, and shipwrecked military personnel at sea** (*Second Convention*).
- **Prisoners of war (POWs)** (*Third Convention*).
- **Civilians, including those in occupied territories** (*Fourth Convention*).

Subsequent protocols extended these protections to cover non-international armed conflicts and prohibited specific weapons and tactics. Together, the Geneva Conventions form a comprehensive legal framework aimed at limiting human suffering during war and safeguarding basic dignity.

Core Principles of the Geneva Conventions

At their heart, the Geneva Conventions are guided by fundamental principles that govern the conduct of armed conflict:

Protection of Civilians: Civilians must not be targeted, and efforts must be made to minimize harm to them. Occupying powers bear responsibility for the welfare of civilian populations under their control.

Humane Treatment of Prisoners of War (POWs): POWs are entitled to humane treatment, including adequate food and medical care. They must not be subjected to torture, degrading treatment, or forced labor.

Safeguarding Medical Personnel and Facilities: Medical personnel, hospitals, and ambulances are protected under the conventions and must not be targeted. The Red Cross emblem symbolizes neutrality and protection.

Prohibition of Inhumane Practices: Acts such as torture, collective punishment, and the use of indiscriminate weapons are explicitly forbidden.

These principles emphasize the distinction between combatants and non-combatants and seek to uphold basic human rights even in the brutality of war.

Applications and Violations in Modern Conflicts

Since their adoption, the Geneva Conventions have been a cornerstone of international law, invoked in numerous conflicts to hold perpetrators accountable and protect vulnerable groups. However, their application has also revealed persistent challenges in enforcement.

Applications: The Geneva Conventions have been effectively applied in conflicts like the Falklands War, the Persian Gulf War, and various peacekeeping missions. Humanitarian organizations, including the ICRC, frequently cite the conventions to advocate for the protection of civilians and the humane treatment of POWs.

Violations: Despite their near-universal acceptance, the Geneva Conventions are often violated with devastating consequences.

✓ In the **Bosnian War**, ethnic cleansing and the deliberate targeting of civilians starkly violated these principles.

✓ During the **Syrian Civil War**, attacks on hospitals and the use of chemical weapons underscored the persistent gap between legal standards and wartime realities.

✓ In the **Russia-Ukraine war**, reports of deliberate attacks on civilian infrastructure, the use of banned weapons, and the mistreatment of prisoners highlight the ongoing challenges in enforcing compliance. These violations call for stronger mechanisms to hold perpetrators accountable and reinforce adherence to international law.

In summary, the Geneva Conventions remain a testament to humanity's aspiration to impose ethical constraints on the horrors of war. They have shaped modern understandings of war crimes and provided a legal framework for holding violators accountable. However, their frequent violations reveal a persistent gap between the ideals of legal standards and the grim realities of modern warfare.

As conflicts like the Russia-Ukraine war continue to challenge these principles, the Geneva Conventions stand as a critical reminder of the international community's responsibility to uphold the rules of humanity. Through vigilance and accountability, the ideals enshrined in these treaties can guide the world toward a more humane approach to conflict, ensuring that even in the darkest times, justice prevails.

1.5 The Rise of Modern Justice: The International Criminal Court (ICC)

The establishment of the International Criminal Court (ICC) marked a transformative moment in the evolution of international justice, addressing critical gaps in the global legal framework for prosecuting war crimes, crimes against humanity, and genocide. As the first permanent international tribunal dedicated to addressing these atrocities, the ICC represents a bold step toward accountability and the rule of law in the face of impunity. However, its journey has been marked by both promise and persistent challenges, reflecting the complexities of enforcing global justice.

The Establishment of the ICC: A Response to Gaps in International Justice

The ICC was established in 2002 through the Rome Statute, a treaty adopted in 1998 by 120 countries. Its creation stemmed from the recognition that ad hoc tribunals, such as those for Rwanda and the former Yugoslavia, while effective in their specific contexts, were limited in scope and duration. The international community envisioned a permanent institution capable of addressing crimes of a similar magnitude, regardless of where they occurred.

Designed as a court of last resort, the ICC steps in when national judicial systems are unwilling or unable to prosecute serious international crimes. Its establishment symbolized a collective commitment to ensuring that perpetrators of the gravest offenses would face justice, closing gaps left by prior mechanisms.

The ICC's Jurisdiction, Mandate, and Notable Cases

The ICC's jurisdiction is defined by the Rome Statute, granting it authority over four major categories of crimes:

- **War crimes:** Violations of the laws of war, such as targeting civilians or using banned weapons.
- **Crimes against humanity:** Systematic or widespread attacks on civilian populations, including acts like enslavement and torture.
- **Genocide:** Acts committed with the intent to destroy, in whole or in part, a national, ethnic, racial, or religious group.
- **The crime of aggression:** Planning or executing acts of aggression that violate the UN Charter.

The court's mandate extends to crimes committed within the territories of member states or by their nationals. However, non-member states, such as the United States, Russia, and China, fall outside its jurisdiction unless referred by the United Nations Security Council (UNSC) or if they voluntarily accept its authority.

Notable cases brought before the ICC illustrate its capacity to address complex atrocities:

- **Thomas Lubanga** (Democratic Republic of Congo): Prosecuted for recruiting child soldiers.
- **Omar al-Bashir** (Sudan): Charged with genocide in Darfur.
- **Dominic Ongwen** (Uganda): Convicted for crimes committed as a commander in the Lord's Resistance Army.

These cases highlight the ICC's ability to bring high-profile offenders to justice but also underscore its reliance on state cooperation for arrests and enforcement.

Challenges Faced by the ICC

Despite its achievements, the ICC faces significant challenges that hinder its effectiveness and expose the intricacies of pursuing justice on a global scale:

Jurisdictional Limitations: The ICC's jurisdiction is restricted to member states and UNSC referrals. This limitation excludes powerful nations like the United States, Russia, and China, which have not ratified the Rome Statute, creating substantial gaps in its reach.

Enforcement Difficulties: Without its own enforcement mechanisms, the ICC relies on member states to arrest suspects and implement rulings. This dependence often leads to delays or failures, especially when political interests conflict with the pursuit of justice.

Accusations of Bias: Critics argue that the ICC disproportionately targets African leaders while overlooking crimes committed by powerful nations or their allies. This perception undermines the court's legitimacy and discourages broader participation.

Geopolitical Pressures: As an independent institution, the ICC must navigate the complexities of international politics. UNSC referrals are subject to vetoes by permanent members, which can block investigations into major conflicts, such as those in Syria or Ukraine.

Resource Constraints: The ICC operates with limited financial and human resources, hampering its ability to investigate and prosecute cases comprehensively and efficiently.

In conclusion, the International Criminal Court represents a significant step forward in the global pursuit of justice, offering a permanent forum to hold perpetrators of the world's gravest crimes accountable. Its establishment reflects a collective aspiration to transcend the limitations of ad hoc tribunals and ensure that justice is not constrained by geography or politics.

However, the ICC's effectiveness depends heavily on the cooperation and political will of the international community. Its challenges, from jurisdictional limitations to accusations of bias, underscore the tension between legal principles and geopolitical realities.

As the Russia-Ukraine war unfolds, the ICC's role in documenting and prosecuting atrocities will serve as a litmus test for its relevance and resilience in addressing modern conflicts. Despite its imperfections, the court remains a vital symbol of humanity's commitment to accountability and the rule of law, reminding the world that, even amid immense challenges, the pursuit of justice is essential.

1.6 Bridging the Past and Present: The Relevance of Historical Frameworks Today

The study of historical frameworks for addressing war crimes is more than a reflection on the past—it is a crucial guide for confronting the challenges of the present. From the Nuremberg Trials to the Geneva Conventions and the establishment of the International Criminal Court (ICC), each milestone underscores humanity's evolving commitment to accountability during conflict. These precedents not only define what constitutes a war crime but also illuminate the mechanisms, successes, and limitations of pursuing justice in even the most complex circumstances.

Historical Milestones and Their Influence on the Russia-Ukraine Conflict

The Russia-Ukraine war serves as a litmus test for the effectiveness of historical frameworks in addressing modern conflicts. Principles established at Nuremberg—namely, that individuals, including state leaders, can be held accountable for their actions—remain central to addressing alleged war crimes in Ukraine. Similarly, the Geneva Conventions provide a robust legal foundation for assessing violations, including attacks on civilians, hospitals, and civilian infrastructure.

The ICC, as the culmination of decades of effort to create a permanent international justice mechanism, offers a pathway to accountability. However, its limitations—such as reliance on state cooperation and lack of jurisdiction over non-member states like Russia—highlight the ongoing tension between the ideals of justice and the realities of international power dynamics.

History reminds us that while legal frameworks are essential, their effectiveness depends on collective will. The Nuremberg Trials succeeded not only because of their legal precedents but also due to the political consensus among Allied powers. In contrast, the lack of such consensus complicates accountability efforts in the Russia-Ukraine war, where geopolitical interests often overshadow legal imperatives.

Connecting Past Mechanisms to Current Challenges

The parallels between historical and contemporary mechanisms of accountability underscore both progress and persistent obstacles. For example:

Documentation of Atrocities: The meticulous documentation of Nazi war crimes during World War II set a gold standard for evidence collection. Today, technologies such as satellite imagery, social media, and forensic tools enhance these capabilities. However, challenges remain in verifying and authenticating evidence in real time, especially in active war zones.

Jurisdictional Constraints: Just as the Nuremberg Trials were limited to prosecuting Axis powers, the ICC faces jurisdictional barriers preventing it from addressing crimes committed by non-member states. This limitation underscores the need for reforms to ensure universal accountability.

Geopolitical Influence: Historical precedents reveal that justice is often shaped by the political dynamics of the time. Selective prosecution of war crimes—whether at Nuremberg, in the Balkans, or in modern conflicts like Syria—demonstrates the enduring struggle to balance legal principles with geopolitical realities.

These connections highlight the relevance of historical frameworks while pointing to areas where improvements are necessary to navigate the complexities of contemporary warfare.

Setting the Stage for Documenting War Crimes

As the Russia-Ukraine conflict unfolds, the practicalities of documenting war crimes become increasingly significant. Gathering evidence, identifying perpetrators, and building cases against them are fraught with challenges, especially amid the chaos of ongoing conflict. Lessons from past efforts emphasize the importance of comprehensive, unbiased, and timely documentation to ensure that justice can be pursued effectively once hostilities cease.

This chapter lays the groundwork for exploring these practicalities in greater detail. The next chapter delves into the tools, methodologies, and ethical considerations involved in investigating war crimes in real time, addressing the delicate balance between evidence collection and the urgent need to provide relief to victims.

In conclusion, bridging the past and present underscores the enduring importance of historical frameworks in shaping the pursuit of justice today. Milestones such as the Nuremberg Trials, the Geneva Conventions, and the creation of the ICC offer valuable lessons for addressing the complexities of modern conflicts like the Russia-Ukraine war. At the same time, these frameworks expose gaps that must be addressed to ensure justice in an increasingly interconnected and politically fragmented world.

Moving forward, the challenge lies in applying these lessons to the practical task of documenting and prosecuting war crimes. By reflecting on the past and adapting to the present, the international community can strive to uphold the ideals of accountability and justice, even amid the uncertainty and devastation of war.

Conclusion: Tracing the Origins of War Crimes

This chapter provided a comprehensive exploration of the historical evolution of war crimes and the frameworks that define and prosecute them. It highlighted humanity's enduring commitment to imposing moral and legal order on the chaos of warfare, tracing this journey through key milestones like ancient codes, the Nuremberg Trials, the Geneva Conventions, and the establishment of the International Criminal Court (ICC).

The chapter underscored how these frameworks shaped modern concepts of accountability and justice, emphasizing their relevance in addressing contemporary conflicts such as the Russia-Ukraine war. It also pointed to persistent challenges, including geopolitical constraints, enforcement difficulties, and the selective application of justice, that continue to test these systems.

The enduring lesson is clear: while these frameworks are not perfect, they remain vital instruments for upholding humanity's values and safeguarding the dignity of those affected by war. By bridging the past and present, this chapter sets the stage for exploring the practicalities of documenting and prosecuting war crimes in ongoing conflicts, where the pursuit of justice faces both unprecedented opportunities and significant obstacles.

2. Unveiling the Truth: Documenting Atrocities

The pursuit of justice begins with the pursuit of truth. In the aftermath of war crimes, documenting atrocities is not merely an act of recording events but a cornerstone of accountability. Building on the frameworks discussed in the previous chapter, this section delves into the practicalities of gathering evidence and uncovering the human cost of war. From survivors recounting their stories to investigators piecing together fragmented evidence, the process of documentation is as complex as it is vital. In an era where technology offers unprecedented tools for capturing the truth, it also presents unique challenges, from verifying authenticity to combating misinformation. As the world confronts conflicts like the Russia-Ukraine war, the task of documenting atrocities remains a pivotal step toward justice, ensuring that the voices of victims are heard and the perpetrators are held accountable.

2.1 From Historical Precedents to Real-Time Challenges

The lessons of history provide a crucial foundation for confronting the evolving realities of modern warfare. The frameworks established through the **Nuremberg Trials**, the **Geneva Conventions**, and the **International Criminal Court** (ICC) demonstrate the enduring power of evidence—whether survivor testimonies, photographs, or official documents—in holding perpetrators accountable and ensuring the voices of victims are not silenced. These milestones set a precedent for justice by showing that thorough documentation is indispensable in achieving accountability. However, as warfare evolves, the task of documenting atrocities has grown more complex, requiring adaptation to real-time challenges.

The Shift to Real-Time Documentation

In contemporary conflicts, such as the **Russia-Ukraine war**, the immediacy of modern technology and the global flow of information have transformed how war crimes are documented. Unlike in the past, where evidence was often collected post-conflict, investigators today work amid active hostilities. This shift necessitates a new level of precision and speed in gathering and verifying evidence, making real-time documentation essential for establishing accountability and preventing further atrocities.

Real-time evidence offers distinct advantages:

- **Strengthening Prosecutions:** Timely documentation provides irrefutable proof of crimes as they occur, bolstering legal cases by capturing details that may fade or be lost over time.
- **Shaping Global Narratives:** Evidence shared immediately raises awareness and mobilizes international pressure, compelling action to protect vulnerable populations and deter violations.

However, the immediacy of real-time documentation presents challenges. Ensuring the credibility of evidence gathered in chaotic environments is a daunting task, compounded by ethical dilemmas in exposing sensitive information while conflicts are still unfolding.

Bridging Historical Lessons and Modern Realities

The growing importance of accurate and timely documentation underscores the need to connect historical precedents with modern realities. The meticulous documentation practices of the Nuremberg Trials taught the world the value of structured, corroborative evidence in delivering justice. Similarly, the Geneva Conventions and ICC guidelines emphasize the critical role of clear, admissible evidence in legal proceedings.

Yet, these lessons must be adapted to meet the demands of 21st-century warfare. Traditional methods of evidence collection, while foundational, must now integrate innovative tools such as satellite imagery, digital forensics, and geospatial analysis to ensure comprehensive and credible documentation. This combination of historical wisdom and modern innovation is essential to uncover the truth, protect victims, and pave the way for justice in the face of contemporary atrocities.

In conclusion, the transition from post-conflict evidence collection to real-time documentation marks a significant evolution in the pursuit of justice. As investigators navigate the complexities of modern conflicts, the need to combine historical lessons with cutting-edge technology becomes increasingly clear. By aligning the past with the present, the global community can ensure that the pursuit of truth and accountability remains steadfast, even amid the chaos of war.

2.2 Voices of the Witnesses: Survivors, Journalists, and Investigators

The pursuit of justice begins with those who bear witness to the horrors of war. Survivors, journalists, and investigators play indispensable roles in documenting atrocities, transforming raw events into actionable evidence and narratives that humanize the devastation. Their collective efforts not only preserve the truth but also lay the foundation for accountability.

Firsthand Accounts from Survivors: Humanizing the Statistics of War

Behind every statistic of war lies a deeply personal story. Survivors—those who have endured unimaginable suffering—offer powerful testimonies that go beyond numbers to reveal the human toll of conflict. Their accounts capture the anguish of lost loved ones, the terror of violence, and the resilience of those who survive. These narratives serve as an essential counterbalance to the abstraction of war, reminding the world that atrocities are not merely violations of law but profound assaults on human dignity.

Survivors' testimonies have historically shaped the course of justice. From Holocaust survivors recounting their experiences at the Nuremberg Trials to victims of ethnic cleansing testifying before modern tribunals, their voices have been instrumental in holding perpetrators accountable. Today, in conflicts like the Russia-Ukraine war, these accounts continue to play a pivotal role, providing irreplaceable insights into crimes that might otherwise remain hidden.

The Indispensable Role of Journalists in Uncovering Hidden Atrocities

Journalists are often the first to bring atrocities to light, venturing into dangerous war zones to report on events the world might otherwise ignore. Armed with cameras, notebooks, and an unwavering commitment to truth, they document the immediate aftermath of attacks, interview survivors, and expose crimes that might otherwise remain buried. Their work not only informs the public but also serves as an essential resource for investigators and legal teams.

Historically, journalists have played a critical role in uncovering war crimes, from exposing the My Lai Massacre in Vietnam to documenting atrocities in Bosnia and Rwanda. In modern conflicts, journalists face unprecedented risks, including targeting by combatants and disinformation campaigns aimed at discrediting their work. Despite these challenges, their efforts remain vital in bridging the gap between conflict zones and the global community, ensuring that the truth reaches those with the power to act.

Investigators on the Frontlines: Building the Foundation for Justice

Investigators, whether affiliated with international bodies, NGOs, or local organizations, are tasked with collecting and verifying evidence of war crimes. Working in active conflict zones, they gather testimonies, analyze physical evidence, and compile reports that form the basis for legal action. Their meticulous work transforms raw accounts into structured cases that can withstand scrutiny in international courts.

Investigators often collaborate with survivors and journalists to build comprehensive narratives of crimes, piecing together timelines, identifying perpetrators, and linking actions to broader patterns of abuse. In conflicts like the Russia-Ukraine war, their work is indispensable in documenting crimes such as the targeting of civilian infrastructure, forced displacements, and the use of banned weapons. The risks they face—ranging from physical danger to psychological trauma—highlight the immense dedication required to pursue justice in the midst of chaos.

Thus, the voices of survivors, journalists, and investigators converge to create a powerful record of truth, humanizing the impact of war while providing the evidence necessary for accountability. Together, they ensure that the atrocities of war are neither forgotten nor ignored, laying the groundwork for a justice that transcends borders and time. Their collective efforts remind the world that even amid the horrors of conflict, the pursuit of truth and justice endures.

2.3 The Digital Era of Accountability: Technology in Evidence Collection

The digital age has revolutionized the way war crimes are documented, offering unprecedented tools for capturing evidence and exposing atrocities. Technology now enables investigators to gather and analyze data in real time, often revealing crimes that would have otherwise gone unnoticed. From satellite imagery to social media, these advancements have reshaped the landscape of accountability, though not without presenting significant challenges and ethical dilemmas.

Satellite Imagery, Drones, and Geospatial Tools: Seeing the Unseen

Satellite imagery and geospatial tools have become invaluable in documenting atrocities from a safe distance, providing irrefutable visual evidence of events on the ground. High-resolution satellite images can reveal mass graves, destroyed villages, or the movement of military equipment, often corroborating survivor testimonies or on-the-ground reports. These tools have been instrumental in conflicts like Syria, where satellite imagery documented the use of chemical weapons and the destruction of civilian infrastructure.

Drones further enhance this capability, offering detailed real-time visuals of conflict zones. They enable investigators to monitor areas inaccessible to traditional methods, capturing evidence of attacks on civilian infrastructure or troop movements. Geospatial analysis, combining data from satellites and drones, allows experts to create comprehensive maps that can link events to specific locations and timelines, strengthening the chain of evidence in legal proceedings.

The Role of Social Media in Documenting and Exposing War Crimes

Social media platforms have emerged as both a tool and a battlefield in the fight for accountability. Videos, photos, and posts shared by individuals in conflict zones often serve as primary evidence, providing real-time insights into war crimes. Platforms like Twitter, Facebook, and TikTok have been used to document everything from indiscriminate bombings to human rights abuses, amplifying the voices of those on the ground.

Citizen journalism, where individuals share unfiltered accounts of events, has democratized the documentation of atrocities. However, the sheer volume of content presents challenges for verification, requiring specialized tools and expertise to confirm authenticity. Organizations like Bellingcat have pioneered methods for verifying user-generated content, demonstrating the potential of social media as a resource for evidence collection.

Limitations and Ethical Considerations in Using Advanced Technologies

While advanced technologies offer unprecedented tools for documenting war crimes, their application is not without significant limitations and ethical dilemmas. As investigators and organizations increasingly rely on these tools, it is crucial to recognize the challenges they present and implement measures to mitigate potential harm.

Challenges in Verification: Ensuring Authenticity

One of the primary challenges in using advanced technologies is verifying the authenticity of digital evidence. Platforms like social media have become valuable sources of real-time information, but they also present a minefield of manipulated content, disinformation campaigns, and unverified claims. For instance, doctored videos, staged photographs, and deepfake technology can blur the line between truth and fabrication, complicating efforts to establish facts.

To address this, investigators must employ rigorous verification processes. Techniques such as metadata analysis, reverse image searches, and geolocation tools are essential for confirming the origin and context of digital content. Organizations like Bellingcat and Amnesty International have set benchmarks for digital forensics, combining human expertise with AI-powered tools to separate authentic evidence from falsehoods. However, even with these advancements, the sheer volume of data can overwhelm investigative teams, delaying justice.

Balancing Privacy and Surveillance

The use of drones, satellites, and other surveillance tools raises important questions about privacy and the rights of individuals in conflict zones. While these technologies can capture invaluable evidence—such as troop movements, mass graves, or destroyed civilian infrastructure—they can also inadvertently violate the privacy and safety of those they aim to protect.

For example, drones equipped with cameras may inadvertently record private moments of civilians, exposing them to potential retaliation or stigma. Similarly, the widespread use of surveillance tools can lead to a perception of intrusion, eroding trust between local communities and investigators. Balancing the need for comprehensive evidence with the ethical imperative to respect privacy requires clear guidelines and safeguards. Limiting access to sensitive footage, anonymizing identifiable data, and obtaining informed consent where possible are steps toward ensuring responsible use.

Selective Documentation: The Risk of Unequal Coverage

Technology often favors areas with robust connectivity and international visibility, inadvertently creating biases in documentation efforts. Conflicts occurring in remote or less connected regions may receive little to no attention, leaving atrocities in these areas undocumented and underrepresented. This selective documentation can distort global narratives, prioritizing some conflicts over others and undermining the principle of equal justice.

To mitigate this, investigators and organizations must strive to allocate resources equitably. Expanding the use of portable technologies, such as mobile apps for field reporting, can help bridge the gap in less accessible areas. Additionally, partnerships with local NGOs and grassroots organizations can enhance documentation efforts in underrepresented regions, ensuring a more comprehensive record of atrocities.

Ethical Imperatives: Protecting Victims and Witnesses

The ethical considerations of using advanced technologies extend beyond the tools themselves to their impact on survivors and witnesses. Publishing sensitive footage or data can expose individuals to retaliation, re-traumatization, or social ostracism. For example, releasing images of mass graves or attacks on civilians may inadvertently identify victims, endangering their families or communities.

To address these risks, investigators must establish robust protocols for the ethical use of technology. This includes anonymizing sensitive data, seeking consent from survivors and witnesses, and carefully weighing the potential harm of publicizing evidence against its value for accountability. Transparency in decision-making and collaboration with human rights experts can further enhance the ethical integrity of documentation efforts.

Thus, advanced technologies are powerful allies in the fight for justice, but their limitations and ethical implications demand careful consideration. By prioritizing rigorous verification processes, respecting privacy, addressing biases in coverage, and protecting those most vulnerable, investigators can harness these tools responsibly. In doing so, they can ensure that technology serves as a force for justice, amplifying truth and accountability without causing unintended harm. As these tools continue to evolve, so too must the standards and practices that guide their use, reinforcing the commitment to a more just and equitable world.

In conclusion, the digital era has brought a wealth of tools for documenting atrocities, offering unprecedented opportunities to uncover the truth and hold perpetrators accountable. However, the effective use of technology in evidence collection requires vigilance, expertise, and ethical considerations. As the world increasingly relies on digital tools to expose war crimes, it must also navigate the complexities they introduce, ensuring that justice remains the guiding principle in this evolving landscape.

2.4 The Fragile Line Between Truth and Fabrication

In the pursuit of justice, the reliability of evidence is paramount. In the chaotic environment of conflict zones, where misinformation and disinformation often thrive, verifying the authenticity of evidence becomes a daunting challenge. The credibility of documentation—whether gathered through testimonies, social media, or advanced technology—plays a critical role in building trust and ensuring accountability. Navigating the fragile line between truth and fabrication requires a meticulous approach that balances urgency with accuracy.

The Challenges of Verifying Evidence in Active Conflict Zones

Active conflict zones present unique obstacles for verifying evidence. Limited access, ongoing violence, and the destruction of physical sites often make direct investigation impossible. In such conditions, reliance on secondary sources, such as digital content or third-party reports, increases. However, these sources can introduce inconsistencies, raising questions about their reliability.

Additionally, the dynamic nature of conflicts means that evidence can quickly degrade or be intentionally destroyed. Perpetrators may actively attempt to conceal their crimes, altering sites or silencing witnesses. Investigators must work against the clock to gather and corroborate evidence, often under immense pressure and in perilous conditions.

Authenticating Digital Evidence: Preventing Misinformation and Disinformation

The rise of digital tools has revolutionized evidence collection but also opened the door to widespread misinformation and disinformation. Images, videos, and reports shared online can be manipulated, making it difficult to distinguish authentic content from fabrications. Sophisticated editing tools and artificial intelligence have further blurred the line between genuine and falsified evidence.

To counter these challenges, investigators rely on advanced techniques for authenticating digital content. Geolocation tools, metadata analysis, and reverse image searches are used to verify the origin and context of online materials. Organizations like Bellingcat and Amnesty International have pioneered methods for forensic analysis of user-generated content, ensuring that only verified evidence is presented in legal or public forums.

However, even verified digital evidence must be handled with caution. Overreliance on online sources risks excluding voices and experiences that are not digitally captured, perpetuating biases in the documentation process.

Building Trust in Documentation to Ensure Accountability

Trust is the cornerstone of effective documentation and accountability. To build trust, evidence collection processes must be transparent, rigorous, and inclusive. Investigators must work to establish the credibility of their methods, ensuring that every piece of evidence can withstand scrutiny in both legal and public spheres.

Engaging with local communities and survivors is essential in this process. Their cooperation and validation can strengthen the authenticity of evidence while fostering a sense of ownership over the pursuit of justice. Similarly, partnerships with independent experts, journalists, and human rights organizations enhance the reliability of documentation efforts.

Trust also hinges on ethical considerations. Respecting the privacy and safety of survivors, avoiding sensationalism, and maintaining impartiality are critical to ensuring that documentation efforts serve justice rather than political or personal agendas.

In summary, the line between truth and fabrication is often thin in the fog of war, but maintaining its integrity is essential for achieving justice. By addressing the challenges of verification, leveraging advanced tools for authentication, and fostering trust through ethical and transparent practices, investigators can ensure that documentation efforts remain credible and impactful. In a world increasingly influenced by digital narratives, the ability to discern truth from fabrication will determine the success of accountability efforts and the enduring strength of justice.

2.5 Setting the Stage for Justice

Documentation of war crimes is more than an act of recording—it is the foundation upon which justice is built. To ensure that future prosecutions are credible and effective, the process of gathering evidence must be unbiased, meticulous, and firmly connected to established international legal frameworks. As investigators navigate the challenges of evidence collection in active conflicts, the balance between urgency and thoroughness becomes critical in setting the stage for accountability.

The Importance of Unbiased Documentation in Ensuring Future Prosecutions

Unbiased documentation is the cornerstone of justice. Evidence must be collected without preconceived conclusions or influence from political agendas to ensure that the process remains impartial and credible. Investigators must focus solely on the facts, allowing the evidence to speak for itself. This impartiality not only strengthens the legal foundation for prosecutions but also builds trust among survivors, communities, and the international audience.

Bias in documentation risks undermining accountability efforts, as courts and international bodies require evidence that is robust, objective, and free from suspicion of manipulation. A single misstep in the documentation process can jeopardize years of work and erode public confidence in the pursuit of justice.

Linking Evidence Collection to International Legal Frameworks Like the ICC

The connection between evidence collection and international legal frameworks, such as the International Criminal Court (ICC), is critical in transforming documentation into actionable cases. The ICC relies on well-documented and verified evidence to pursue cases of war crimes, crimes against humanity, and genocide. Therefore, investigators must align their methods with the legal standards required by these institutions.

This alignment involves collecting evidence that meets the criteria of admissibility and relevance under international law. Metadata from digital evidence, chain-of-custody protocols for physical artifacts, and corroborative testimonies all contribute to building strong cases that can withstand legal scrutiny. By linking documentation efforts to these frameworks, investigators ensure that their work contributes meaningfully to justice, rather than remaining a collection of unconnected data.

Conclusion

This chapter has provided a detailed exploration of the multifaceted process of documenting atrocities, emphasizing its critical role in achieving accountability. From the personal testimonies of survivors to the advanced capabilities of modern technology, the chapter highlights how these tools and narratives collectively ensure the preservation of truth and justice.

While the digital era offers unprecedented opportunities for evidence collection, it also presents challenges, including verifying authenticity, addressing misinformation, and navigating ethical considerations. By combining historical lessons with modern innovations, investigators and organizations can navigate these complexities to build robust cases that withstand legal scrutiny and foster public trust.

Documenting atrocities is not merely an administrative or technical task—it is a moral responsibility. It serves as the foundation for accountability, a safeguard for justice, and a beacon of hope for victims and survivors. As the world continues to confront the realities of conflict, these efforts remind us that even in the darkest times, the pursuit of truth and justice can endure.

3. A Global Legal Framework Under Pressure

In the pursuit of justice for war crimes and atrocities, the global legal framework serves as both a beacon of hope and a reflection of its challenges. Building on the evidence collected through rigorous documentation, international law provides the mechanisms to hold perpetrators accountable and uphold the principles of humanity. Yet, as modern conflicts grow more complex, this framework faces increasing strain. Powerful nations exert disproportionate influence, geopolitical rivalries undermine impartiality, and unconventional warfare tests the adaptability of existing legal norms. This chapter explores the fragile state of global justice, examining how international law operates under pressure, the role of institutions like the ICC and UN, and the enduring tension between state sovereignty and global accountability.

3.1 Building on Documentation: From Evidence to Action

The documentation of atrocities is the first, vital step in the journey toward justice, but its true value lies in its ability to catalyze legal action. As evidence moves from conflict zones to international legal institutions, it becomes the foundation upon which cases are built, ensuring that those responsible for war crimes are held accountable. This section explores how the painstaking work of documenting atrocities transitions into actionable justice, bridging the gap between the field and the courtroom.

Connecting Documentation to Justice

Every piece of evidence—whether survivor testimony, satellite imagery, or physical artifacts—serves a dual purpose: preserving the truth and enabling prosecution. Documentation efforts, as explored in the previous chapter, lay the groundwork by capturing the scope and scale of atrocities, identifying perpetrators, and establishing patterns of abuse. When meticulously collected, this evidence not only humanizes the impact of war but also serves as irrefutable proof of crimes committed.

The transition from documentation to justice begins with translating raw data into structured legal arguments. Investigators work closely with legal experts to ensure that evidence aligns with the standards of international law, such as those set by the **International Criminal Court** (ICC) or regional tribunals. This alignment ensures that the documented atrocities are not only compelling but also admissible in legal proceedings.

How Evidence Feeds into International Legal Mechanisms

For international legal institutions like the ICC, evidence serves as the cornerstone of justice. The process typically involves several key stages:

Collection and Verification: Field investigators gather evidence, which is then scrutinized for authenticity and relevance. Verification methods, such as geolocation tools or forensic analysis, strengthen the reliability of the material.

Analysis and Compilation: Legal teams analyze the evidence to build comprehensive case files. This process often involves creating timelines, mapping patterns of abuse, and linking individuals or groups to specific crimes.

Presentation in Court: The compiled evidence is presented in trials, where it must withstand rigorous scrutiny. Strong documentation increases the likelihood of convictions by demonstrating a clear connection between the crime and the accused.

International mechanisms rely heavily on this chain of evidence to overcome the challenges posed by distance, time, and geopolitical complexities. Without robust documentation, many cases would falter due to insufficient proof or lack of jurisdictional clarity.

Bridging the Gap Between Fieldwork and Legal Action

Despite its importance, the journey from fieldwork to courtroom is fraught with obstacles. Field investigators often operate under perilous conditions, navigating active conflict zones and limited access. Meanwhile, legal institutions face hurdles such as bureaucratic delays, jurisdictional disputes, and political interference.

To bridge this gap, collaboration between investigators, human rights organizations, and international legal bodies is essential. Sharing resources, expertise, and data ensures that evidence collected in the field seamlessly integrates into legal frameworks. Additionally, fostering trust and communication between local communities and international institutions strengthens the legitimacy and impact of justice efforts.

Technological advancements also play a critical role in this process. Digital tools, such as blockchain for evidence storage or AI-powered analysis, enhance the efficiency and accuracy of transitioning evidence from documentation to prosecution. These innovations not only streamline the process but also ensure that evidence remains secure and tamper-proof throughout its journey.

In summary, the journey from documenting atrocities to achieving justice is a complex but indispensable process in the global fight against impunity. By connecting the meticulous efforts of field investigators with the rigorous demands of legal institutions, the world can ensure that evidence collected in the most challenging circumstances leads to meaningful accountability. As this chapter continues, we will explore the broader frameworks of international law and the institutions that rely on this evidence to uphold the principles of justice in an increasingly polarized world.

3.2 International Law in the Face of Modern Conflicts

International law has long served as the backbone of efforts to regulate the conduct of war and hold perpetrators of atrocities accountable. However, as modern conflicts evolve in complexity and scale, the frameworks of international law are increasingly tested. From addressing the realities of hybrid warfare to adapting to the rise of unconventional tactics, international humanitarian and criminal law must continuously evolve to remain relevant and effective.

The Evolution of International Law to Address Contemporary Warfare

The foundations of international law in wartime were laid with treaties like the **Geneva Conventions** and the establishment of the **International Criminal Court (ICC)**. These frameworks codified principles that sought to limit the horrors of war, protect non-combatants, and ensure accountability for violations. Over the decades, these principles have been expanded and adapted to reflect the changing nature of conflict, such as the inclusion of protections for civilians in occupied territories and the prohibition of chemical and biological weapons.

However, contemporary warfare introduces challenges that these frameworks were not initially designed to address. Cyber warfare, drone strikes, and proxy conflicts blur the lines between combatants and civilians, raising questions about how existing laws apply. Additionally, non-state actors, such as terrorist organizations and private military contractors, operate outside the traditional state-centric model of war, complicating efforts to enforce international law.

Key Principles of International Humanitarian and Criminal Law

At the core of international law are principles that aim to mitigate the impact of war and hold violators accountable:

Distinction: Parties to a conflict must distinguish between combatants and civilians, ensuring that civilians are not targeted.

Proportionality: The use of force must be proportional to the military advantage sought, avoiding excessive harm to civilians and infrastructure.

Necessity: Military actions must be necessary to achieve legitimate objectives, minimizing harm whenever possible.

Accountability: Individuals responsible for war crimes, crimes against humanity, or genocide must be held accountable through legal mechanisms, regardless of rank or position.

These principles are enshrined in treaties like the Geneva Conventions and guided by the Rome Statute, which established the ICC. However, their implementation often depends on the willingness of states and international bodies to act decisively, a challenge exacerbated by modern conflicts.

Challenges Posed by Unconventional and Hybrid Warfare

The rise of unconventional and hybrid warfare presents significant challenges to the application and enforcement of international law:

Blurred Lines Between Combatants and Civilians: In hybrid warfare, tactics such as cyberattacks, disinformation campaigns, and the use of irregular forces complicate the identification of combatants. Civilians may be co-opted into military efforts, either willingly or under duress, challenging the principle of distinction.

Non-State Actors: The increasing role of non-state actors, such as armed groups, terrorist organizations, and private military contractors, disrupts traditional legal frameworks. These entities often operate outside the jurisdiction of international treaties, making accountability difficult.

Technology and Asymmetric Warfare: The use of drones, autonomous weapons, and cyber tools raises new ethical and legal questions. For example, how should responsibility be assigned for a drone strike gone wrong, or a cyberattack that disables critical civilian infrastructure?

State Sovereignty vs. Global Accountability: The principle of state sovereignty often conflicts with international efforts to enforce accountability. Powerful nations may resist external scrutiny or shield allies from legal consequences, undermining the credibility of international law.

Thus, international law remains a critical tool for addressing the atrocities of war, but its frameworks must continue to evolve to meet the challenges of modern conflicts. The principles of distinction, proportionality, and accountability provide a moral compass, but their enforcement requires a collective commitment to justice and adaptability to new forms of warfare. As the chapter progresses, we will examine how international institutions navigate these complexities, balancing the demands of state sovereignty with the need for global accountability in an increasingly interconnected and polarized world.

3.3 The Power Dynamics of Global Justice

The enforcement of international law and the pursuit of global justice are inextricably linked to the power dynamics among nations. While international humanitarian and criminal law is built on principles of fairness and accountability, the practical application of these ideals is often shaped by the interests of the most powerful states. Geopolitical agendas, selective enforcement, and unequal application of justice erode the credibility of international mechanisms and challenge the foundational ideals of impartiality and fairness.

How Powerful Nations Shape International Law Enforcement

Powerful nations wield considerable influence over the enforcement of international law, often dictating the scope and focus of accountability efforts. This influence manifests in several key ways:

Control Over International Institutions: As permanent members of the United Nations Security Council (UNSC), nations such as the United States, Russia, and China possess veto power, enabling them to block resolutions or investigations that conflict with their strategic interests. For instance, UNSC referrals to the International Criminal Court (ICC) often reflect geopolitical calculations rather than impartial considerations of justice.

Bilateral Pressures: Powerful states frequently leverage their influence to shape the behavior of weaker nations, aligning outcomes of investigations or judicial cooperation with their political goals. These pressures can deter impartial investigations and hinder international accountability.

Creation of Ad Hoc Tribunals: Ad hoc tribunals, such as those for Rwanda and the former Yugoslavia, have successfully prosecuted war crimes, but their establishment and scope often depend on the approval and funding of influential nations. This dependence can limit their jurisdiction to strategically significant conflicts while sidelining others.

The Impact of Geopolitical Interests on Accountability Efforts

Geopolitical interests frequently undermine the impartiality of international justice, leading to accusations of bias and double standards. Nations may selectively support justice initiatives that align with their foreign policy objectives while obstructing those that implicate their allies or expose their own actions.

Selective Prosecutions: The ICC has faced criticism for disproportionately targeting African leaders while avoiding cases involving powerful nations or their allies. This perception of selective justice has fueled distrust among developing nations and prompted calls for reforms to address jurisdictional and operational biases.

Shielding Allies: In conflicts where powerful nations have vested interests, accountability efforts are often obstructed. For example, international responses to alleged war crimes in Yemen have been complicated by the involvement of influential states providing military support to the parties in conflict.

Inconsistent Interventions: Geopolitical calculations frequently determine the intensity and timing of international responses. Atrocities in some regions prompt swift action, while others are met with indifference or delays, undermining the credibility of international justice mechanisms.

Examples of Selective Justice and Its Implications for Global Trust

Instances of selective justice underscore the challenges of achieving universal accountability and highlight the erosion of trust in global institutions:

The Iraq War (2003): Despite widespread allegations of international law violations, including the use of torture and civilian casualties, no significant legal actions were taken against coalition forces, leading to accusations of hypocrisy.

The Syria Conflict: Geopolitical rivalries, particularly between the United States and Russia, have hindered meaningful accountability for atrocities committed during the Syrian Civil War. This deadlock has left victims without recourse and emboldened perpetrators.

The Ukraine Crisis: While international attention on alleged war crimes in the Russia-Ukraine conflict has been substantial, critics argue that similar atrocities in less geopolitically significant regions, such as Yemen or the Tigray region in Ethiopia, receive far less scrutiny or support.

These examples highlight how selective justice weakens the legitimacy of international mechanisms and fosters cynicism among nations and communities seeking redress. The perception that global justice serves the interests of the powerful rather than universal principles of accountability risks eroding the very foundations of fairness.

In conclusion, the power dynamics of global justice reveal a troubling tension between the ideals of impartiality and the realities of geopolitics. While international law aspires to hold all perpetrators accountable, its enforcement often mirrors the strategic interests of the most influential nations. Addressing these imbalances is essential for restoring trust in global institutions and ensuring that justice becomes a force for equality, not a tool of power. As the chapter progresses, we will explore how key institutions, such as the ICC and UN, navigate these challenges and uphold the principles of accountability in an increasingly polarized world.

3.4 Pillars of Global Justice: The ICC, UN, and Regional Courts

The global legal framework for addressing war crimes and atrocities rests on three institutional pillars: the **International Criminal Court (ICC)**, the **United Nations (UN)**, and **regional courts**. Each plays a distinct role in upholding accountability and justice, forming a system designed to respond to violations of international law. However, these institutions operate under varying mandates, successes, and limitations, reflecting both the strengths and vulnerabilities of the global justice system.

The International Criminal Court: Jurisdiction, Successes, and Limitations

The ICC is the first permanent international tribunal dedicated to prosecuting individuals for war crimes, crimes against humanity, genocide, and the crime of aggression. Established through the **Rome Statute of 1998**, the court seeks to address cases where national judicial systems are unable or unwilling to act.

Jurisdiction: The ICC's jurisdiction covers crimes committed within the territories of its member states or by their nationals. Cases can also be referred by the UN Security Council (UNSC) or accepted voluntarily by non-member states. However, the refusal of powerful nations like the United States, Russia, and China to ratify the Rome Statute significantly limits the court's reach.

Successes: The ICC has achieved notable milestones, including the conviction of **Thomas Lubanga** for recruiting child soldiers in the Democratic Republic of Congo and **Dominic Ongwen**, a former commander of the Lord's Resistance Army in Uganda. These cases highlight the court's ability to address severe violations and deliver justice to victims.

Limitations: Despite its successes, the ICC faces several challenges:

✓ **Enforcement:** The ICC relies on member states to arrest and extradite suspects, limiting its capacity to act independently.

✓ **Selective Justice:** Perceptions of bias, particularly its focus on African leaders, have undermined the court's legitimacy.

✓ **Geopolitical Pressures:** UNSC referrals are subject to vetoes by powerful nations, restricting the court's ability to address politically sensitive conflicts.

The Role of the United Nations in Maintaining Global Accountability

The UN serves as a central coordinator of international efforts to uphold accountability and prevent impunity. Its mechanisms, including fact-finding missions and peacekeeping operations, complement the work of the ICC and regional courts.

Fact-Finding and Investigations: The UN deploys fact-finding missions to conflict zones to document atrocities and gather evidence. For example, the **Independent International Commission of Inquiry on Syria** has produced critical reports on violations during the Syrian Civil War, shaping international responses and informing legal proceedings.

UN Security Council Referrals: The UNSC can refer cases to the ICC, as demonstrated by the referral of Sudan's **Omar al-Bashir** for crimes in Darfur. However, the veto power of permanent members often obstructs referrals in politically sensitive conflicts, such as those in Syria or Yemen.

Challenges: The UN's effectiveness is constrained by geopolitical rivalries, funding limitations, and its reliance on state cooperation. Balancing state sovereignty with the need for accountability remains a persistent challenge, complicating efforts to address global injustices.

Regional Courts and Their Contributions to Localized Justice

Regional courts and tribunals address conflicts with localized implications, often combining international legal standards with cultural and historical contexts to deliver justice that resonates with affected communities. However, their impact is frequently hindered by resource constraints and political interference.

Notable Regional Courts:

✓ **European Court of Human Rights (ECHR):** The ECHR has addressed human rights violations across Europe, such as in *Alekseyev v. Russia*, where it ruled against Russia for violating LGBTQ+ rights. However, enforcement relies on member state compliance, which is inconsistent.

✓ **African Court on Human and Peoples' Rights:** In *Tanganyika Law Society v. Tanzania*, the court ruled against restrictive election laws, promoting democratic principles. Yet, political resistance from several African nations undermines its jurisdiction.

✓ **Inter-American Court of Human Rights:** The court's ruling in *Velásquez Rodríguez v. Honduras* set a standard for addressing forced disappearances during military dictatorships in Latin America. However, political interference and non-compliance by states remain significant challenges.

Localized Tribunals:

✓ **Special Court for Sierra Leone:** Successfully prosecuted leaders of Sierra Leone's civil war, including Charles Taylor. However, funding limitations and jurisdictional constraints reduced its scope.

✓ **Extraordinary Chambers in the Courts of Cambodia (ECCC):** Convicted senior Khmer Rouge leaders for genocide and crimes against humanity. Despite successes, the tribunal has faced criticism for its high costs and lengthy trials, eroding public confidence.

Challenges and Limitations:

✓ **Resource Constraints:** Many regional courts lack adequate funding, limiting their investigative and prosecutorial capabilities.

✓ **Political Interference:** Governments often resist adverse rulings, undermining the authority of these courts.

✓ **Jurisdictional Challenges:** Compliance with rulings is inconsistent, as regional courts lack binding enforcement mechanisms.

Public Perception: Delays and limited outcomes, such as the ECCC's few convictions after years of proceedings, diminish trust in these institutions.

Thus, the ICC, UN, and regional courts form the backbone of the global justice system, each contributing uniquely to the pursuit of accountability. While these institutions have achieved significant successes, they face substantial challenges, including resource constraints, political interference, and perceptions of bias. Strengthening coordination among these pillars, addressing their limitations, and promoting equitable reforms are essential to ensure that justice remains accessible, impartial, and effective. As the chapter progresses, attention will shift to the broader challenges of maintaining justice in a polarized world and the steps needed to reinforce these pillars for future conflicts.

3.5 The Fragility of Justice in a Polarized World

In an increasingly polarized world, the fragility of international legal institutions has become a pressing concern. Designed to uphold accountability and justice, these institutions now face mounting challenges from political divisions, competing national interests, and the erosion of trust in global systems. Balancing the sovereignty of states with the demand for international accountability requires resilience, adaptability, and a collective commitment to justice.

The Risks of Undermining International Legal Institutions

The credibility of international legal institutions, such as the **International Criminal Court (ICC)** and the **United Nations (UN)**, is essential for maintaining global accountability. However, these institutions are frequently undermined by systemic vulnerabilities and external pressures:

Political Interference: Powerful nations manipulate or obstruct the functioning of legal mechanisms to shield themselves or their allies from scrutiny. This interference weakens the perception of impartiality and undermines the legitimacy of international justice.

Non-Cooperation: Countries that refuse to recognize or cooperate with international bodies, such as non-signatories to the Rome Statute, limit the jurisdiction and effectiveness of institutions like the ICC. This lack of cooperation creates significant gaps in accountability.

Resource Constraints: Inadequate funding and staffing hinder the ability of international institutions to investigate, prosecute, and enforce rulings effectively. These constraints slow down the judicial process and diminish the ability to respond to emerging conflicts.

Such vulnerabilities create a cycle of diminished authority and reduced trust. As these institutions falter, perpetrators of atrocities are emboldened, and victims are left without recourse, eroding the foundations of global justice.

Balancing State Sovereignty with the Demand for Global Accountability

One of the most persistent challenges in international law is reconciling state sovereignty with the need for accountability in an interconnected world. While sovereignty remains a cornerstone of international relations, it often conflicts with efforts to address war crimes, crimes against humanity, and genocide.

Sovereignty as a Shield: States frequently invoke sovereignty to resist external interventions, even when evidence of atrocities is overwhelming. This resistance can delay or obstruct justice, leaving victims without recourse and fostering impunity.

The Need for Accountability: Global accountability mechanisms are essential for deterring future crimes and delivering justice to victims. Balancing these mechanisms with respect for sovereignty requires innovative approaches, such as strengthening regional courts and fostering voluntary cooperation with international bodies.

The Principle of Complementarity: The ICC operates on the principle of complementarity, intervening only when national judicial systems are unwilling or unable to act. This principle underscores the importance of empowering domestic courts to handle cases, while maintaining the ICC as a safety net for justice. Strengthening national judicial systems can reduce dependency on international bodies and enhance the overall effectiveness of global accountability efforts.

In conclusion, the fragility of international legal institutions reflects the challenges of navigating a polarized and interconnected world. Political interference, non-cooperation, and resource constraints threaten their ability to deliver justice and uphold accountability. Addressing these issues requires a concerted effort to strengthen the independence and capacity of global institutions while promoting respect for their rulings.

Balancing state sovereignty with global accountability is a delicate but necessary task. By empowering domestic courts, enhancing regional mechanisms, and ensuring the ICC remains a reliable safety net, the international community can build a more resilient and equitable system of justice. This section sets the stage for exploring actionable strategies to reinforce the global legal framework and ensure it can address the complexities of modern conflicts.

Conclusion: A Global Legal Framework Under Pressure

This chapter examined the global justice system's strengths and vulnerabilities, highlighting its critical role in addressing war crimes and atrocities. From the meticulous transition of evidence into legal action to the complexities of international law and the influence of geopolitical power dynamics, this chapter demonstrated how the pursuit of justice operates under immense pressure.

The discussion of institutions such as the ICC, the UN, and regional courts revealed both their successes and the limitations they face, including jurisdictional challenges, political interference, and resource constraints. Despite these hurdles, these pillars of global justice remain essential for upholding accountability and advancing the principles of humanity.

However, the fragility of international legal institutions underscores the need for resilience and reform. Balancing state sovereignty with the demand for global accountability requires innovative strategies that empower domestic courts, strengthen regional mechanisms, and enhance the effectiveness of international bodies like the ICC and UN.

As the global community confronts the realities of modern conflicts, this chapter sets the stage for actionable strategies to reinforce the global legal framework. Ensuring justice in a polarized world demands collective resolve, adaptability, and a commitment to the ideals of fairness and accountability. Let the lessons from this exploration guide the international community toward a more robust and equitable system of justice.

4. Russia and Ukraine: A Case Study in Accountability

The Russia-Ukraine conflict stands as a stark reminder of the complexities and challenges of pursuing justice in the midst of war. As the first major interstate conflict in Europe since the Balkan wars, it has not only caused immense human suffering but also raised critical questions about the effectiveness of global accountability mechanisms. Allegations of war crimes, including attacks on civilians, forced deportations, and the destruction of civilian infrastructure, have thrust the conflict into the spotlight of international law. This chapter delves into the key allegations of war crimes, examines the international community's response, and explores the diplomatic and legal hurdles in prosecuting nations during an active conflict. By analyzing this case, we aim to uncover the broader implications for the global pursuit of justice.

4.1 Context and Background: The Russia-Ukraine Conflict

The Russia-Ukraine conflict is both a humanitarian tragedy and a geopolitical flashpoint, revealing the complexities of accountability in a modern war. Understanding the context and background of this conflict is essential to comprehending the allegations of war crimes and the challenges of pursuing justice in real time. Rooted in historical tensions and fueled by contemporary geopolitical dynamics, the war has not only disrupted the region but also tested the resilience of global legal frameworks.

Historical and Geopolitical Roots of the Conflict

The origins of the Russia-Ukraine conflict trace back to a long and turbulent history of cultural, political, and territorial disputes. Following the dissolution of the Soviet Union in 1991, Ukraine emerged as an independent state, yet its ties to Russia remained complex. Tensions escalated in 2014 when Russia annexed Crimea, a move widely condemned as a violation of international law. The annexation was accompanied by the emergence of pro-Russian separatist movements in Eastern Ukraine, sparking a low-intensity conflict that laid the groundwork for the full-scale invasion in February 2022.

Geopolitically, the conflict is shaped by Ukraine's aspirations to align with the West, including its pursuit of closer ties with NATO and the European Union. Russia views these moves as threats to its sphere of influence, framing its actions as defensive. This intersection of historical grievances and strategic concerns has created a volatile environment where diplomacy has repeatedly failed.

Key Events Leading to Allegations of War Crimes

The escalation of the conflict in 2022 brought with it widespread allegations of war crimes. Reports of indiscriminate shelling of civilian areas, attacks on hospitals, and the use of cluster munitions have drawn global condemnation. Specific incidents, such as the bombing of a theater in Mariupol sheltering civilians and the mass killings in Bucha, have become emblematic of the brutality of the conflict.

The use of tactics that target civilian populations, forced deportations to Russian-controlled territories, and the destruction of critical infrastructure have raised concerns about violations of international humanitarian law. Investigative bodies, including the United Nations and independent NGOs, have documented these allegations, calling for accountability even as the conflict continues.

Overview of the Humanitarian Impact on Civilians

The human cost of the Russia-Ukraine war is staggering. Millions of Ukrainians have been displaced, with many seeking refuge in neighboring countries. Civilian casualties continue to mount, exacerbated by attacks on residential areas, schools, and healthcare facilities. Access to basic necessities, such as food, water, and medical care, has been severely disrupted in war-torn regions, creating a humanitarian crisis of immense proportions.

Beyond the immediate physical toll, the psychological trauma inflicted on civilians, particularly children, is profound. Families torn apart, communities uprooted, and the constant threat of violence have left lasting scars on the affected population. Humanitarian organizations face immense challenges in delivering aid amid active hostilities, further compounding the suffering of those caught in the crossfire.

Thus, the Russia-Ukraine conflict, with its historical roots, strategic dimensions, and devastating human impact, serves as a critical case study for examining accountability during an active war. As the chapter progresses, we will explore the allegations of war crimes in greater detail, analyze the international community's response, and uncover the broader implications for the global pursuit of justice. By contextualizing the conflict, we can better understand the stakes involved and the urgent need for robust accountability mechanisms.

4.2 Allegations of War Crimes: A Closer Look

Allegations of war crimes in the Russia-Ukraine conflict have drawn global attention, underscoring the gravity of the atrocities committed and the urgent need for accountability. Documented instances of civilian targeting, forced deportations, and the destruction of vital infrastructure have painted a grim picture of human suffering. Compounding these violations are reports of the use of prohibited weapons and other breaches of international law, raising critical questions about adherence to the principles of humanitarian law. In this section, we delve deeper into these allegations and examine the role of technology and media in uncovering and documenting these crimes.

Documented Cases of Civilian Targeting, Forced Deportations, and Infrastructure Destruction

The Russia-Ukraine war has been marked by numerous reports of civilian populations being deliberately targeted, a blatant violation of international humanitarian law. Specific incidents, such as the bombing of a theater in Mariupol that sheltered hundreds of civilians and the shelling of maternity hospitals, have shocked the world. Investigative reports have documented the deliberate targeting of civilian infrastructure, including schools, power grids, and water supplies, leaving communities without basic necessities and exposing vulnerable populations to extreme hardship.

Forced deportations, particularly of Ukrainian children to Russian-controlled territories, represent another troubling aspect of the conflict. International organizations, including the United Nations, have raised alarms about the displacement of families and the separation of children, actions that may constitute crimes against humanity. These practices not only devastate lives but also aim to erode cultural and national identities, deepening the psychological wounds of war.

Use of Prohibited Weapons and Other Violations of International Law

Reports of the use of cluster munitions and thermobaric weapons in civilian areas have further amplified concerns about violations of international law. These weapons, known for their indiscriminate and devastating effects, have caused widespread destruction and loss of life, undermining the principles of distinction and proportionality enshrined in the Geneva Conventions.

Additionally, allegations of sexual violence, torture of prisoners, and the mistreatment of detainees have emerged, highlighting the pervasive nature of the violations. Investigators have documented mass graves and evidence of summary executions in liberated areas, such as Bucha, providing chilling insight into the extent of the atrocities. These actions violate not only international humanitarian law but also the fundamental tenets of human rights, calling for swift and decisive accountability measures.

The Role of Technology and Media in Bringing These Atrocities to Light

Technology and media have played an instrumental role in documenting and exposing the atrocities committed during the Russia-Ukraine conflict. Satellite imagery has provided visual evidence of destroyed cities, mass graves, and troop movements, offering irrefutable proof of violations. Drone footage has captured real-time destruction and attacks on civilian infrastructure, while geolocation and timestamping tools have enabled investigators to verify the authenticity of digital evidence.

Social media platforms have become critical avenues for citizen journalism, with individuals in conflict zones sharing videos, photos, and testimonies that reveal the human cost of the war. Organizations like Bellingcat and Amnesty International have utilized open-source intelligence (OSINT) to corroborate these reports, bridging the gap between digital documentation and legal accountability.

However, the digital era also presents challenges, including the spread of misinformation and the manipulation of evidence. Investigators must navigate these pitfalls to ensure that the evidence presented is credible, reliable, and admissible in legal proceedings.

In summary, the allegations of war crimes in the Russia-Ukraine conflict highlight the depth of human suffering and the urgency of addressing violations of international law. From civilian targeting to the use of prohibited weapons, these actions underscore the need for robust mechanisms to hold perpetrators accountable. Technology and media, while invaluable in shedding light on these atrocities, must be wielded responsibly to strengthen the pursuit of justice. As this chapter progresses, we will examine how the international community has responded to these allegations and the challenges of ensuring accountability in an active war.

4.3 The International Community's Response

The international community's response to the Russia-Ukraine conflict underscores the urgency and complexity of addressing war crimes during active hostilities. Institutions like the **International Criminal Court (ICC)** and the **United Nations (UN)** have taken significant steps to investigate and document atrocities, while humanitarian organizations play a critical role in gathering evidence and advocating for accountability. At the same time, diplomatic efforts reveal both the potential and limitations of collective action in ensuring justice and deterring further violations.

Actions by International Bodies: The ICC and UN

International institutions have been at the forefront of responding to allegations of war crimes in the Russia-Ukraine conflict. The ICC launched a formal investigation shortly after the full-scale invasion in February 2022, prioritizing crimes such as deliberate attacks on civilians, forced deportations, and the use of prohibited weapons. The court has issued arrest warrants and initiated evidence-gathering missions, aiming to build a robust legal foundation for prosecuting those responsible. Despite these efforts, the ICC's lack of enforcement mechanisms limits its ability to act against powerful non-member states like Russia.

The UN has mobilized various resources to address the conflict. The **Independent International Commission of Inquiry on Ukraine**, established by the Human Rights Council, has documented violations of international humanitarian law, including attacks on civilian infrastructure, mass killings, and forced displacements. These findings provide critical inputs for global accountability mechanisms and inform policy decisions by member states. However, the UN's effectiveness is constrained by geopolitical dynamics, including the veto power wielded by Russia as a permanent member of the UN Security Council.

The Role of Humanitarian Organizations in Documenting and Advocating for Accountability

Humanitarian organizations have been instrumental in documenting the human cost of the conflict and advocating for justice. Groups such as **Amnesty International**, **Human Rights Watch**, and the **International Committee of the Red Cross (ICRC)** have played pivotal roles in:

✓ **Evidence Collection:** Gathering testimonies, analyzing the use of prohibited weapons, and highlighting attacks on civilian infrastructure.

✓ **Raising Awareness:** Amplifying the voices of victims through reports and campaigns, pressuring governments and international institutions to act.

For example, Amnesty International's documentation of atrocities in cities like Mariupol and Bucha has galvanized calls for independent investigations and stronger sanctions against perpetrators. These organizations often operate in dangerous environments, facing restricted access to conflict zones and the threat of retaliation. Despite these risks, their work remains indispensable for holding perpetrators accountable and supporting justice initiatives.

Global Diplomatic Responses and Their Effectiveness

Diplomatic efforts to address the Russia-Ukraine conflict have been multifaceted, encompassing sanctions, military aid, and judicial cooperation. Western nations, led by the United States and the European Union, have coordinated economic measures to weaken Russia's capacity to wage war. These include:

✓ **Sanctions:** Freezing assets, banning exports of critical technologies, and targeting individuals implicated in war crimes.

✓ **Military and Humanitarian Aid:** Providing equipment, training, and financial support to bolster Ukraine's defense and address humanitarian needs.

International coalitions, such as the **Joint Investigation Team (JIT)**, have supported Ukraine's efforts to document atrocities and strengthen its judicial capacity. The JIT's cross-border cooperation exemplifies how regional initiatives can complement global mechanisms by addressing jurisdictional and logistical challenges.

However, the effectiveness of these responses is mixed. While sanctions and aid demonstrate solidarity, they have not deterred ongoing violations. Geopolitical divisions within the international community, particularly between Western nations and countries sympathetic to Russia, hinder unified action. Russia's veto power in the UN Security Council has blocked critical resolutions, highlighting the limitations of existing diplomatic mechanisms.

In conclusion, the international community's response to the Russia-Ukraine conflict reflects a determined but constrained effort to address the unprecedented challenges of pursuing accountability during an active war. While institutions like the ICC and UN, along with humanitarian organizations, have made significant strides in documenting and advocating for justice, their impact is tempered by geopolitical realities, enforcement limitations, and diplomatic fractures. Moving forward, innovative approaches and stronger international collaboration will be essential to ensure justice and accountability in this and future conflicts.

4.4 Challenges in Prosecuting War Crimes During an Active Conflict

Prosecuting war crimes during an active conflict is fraught with challenges, spanning legal, diplomatic, and practical dimensions. The ongoing hostilities in the Russia-Ukraine war magnify these difficulties, as the international community grapples with pursuing justice amid the chaos of war. This section examines the obstacles that hinder accountability efforts, from navigating diplomatic and legal barriers to the complexities of evidence collection and the political implications of holding a major power accountable.

Diplomatic and Legal Obstacles to Initiating Prosecutions

Bringing war crimes to trial during an ongoing conflict requires overcoming a labyrinth of diplomatic and legal hurdles. Key obstacles include:

State Sovereignty: Nations frequently invoke sovereignty to resist external interventions, complicating efforts by international bodies like the ICC. In Russia's case, its refusal to recognize ICC jurisdiction and its veto power on the UN Security Council (UNSC) create significant barriers to initiating legal actions.

Immunity of State Leaders: International law often protects sitting heads of state and high-ranking officials from prosecution, shielding key decision-makers from accountability during the conflict. This immunity can delay or derail justice efforts until political circumstances change.

Lack of Precedent for Active War Prosecutions: While post-conflict tribunals, such as those for Rwanda and the former Yugoslavia, have effectively addressed war crimes, prosecuting such crimes in real-time is rare and logistically complex. This lack of precedent adds uncertainty to legal proceedings and slows the pursuit of justice.

These obstacles not only delay accountability but also erode public confidence in the effectiveness of international law to address urgent crises.

Issues with Evidence Collection and Witness Protection Amid Ongoing Hostilities

Gathering and preserving evidence during an active conflict is a dangerous and resource-intensive process. Investigators face a range of challenges that hinder their ability to build robust cases:

Access to Conflict Zones: Active hostilities make it nearly impossible for investigators to access affected areas, secure crime scenes, and collect physical evidence. Key sites, such as mass graves or bombed civilian infrastructure, may remain inaccessible or be destroyed, complicating documentation efforts.

Witness Protection: Witnesses willing to testify face significant risks, including retaliation, intimidation, or displacement. Ensuring their safety during an active conflict is particularly challenging, often deterring individuals from coming forward or jeopardizing the reliability of their testimonies.

Degradation of Evidence: In war-torn areas, the destruction of infrastructure and the passage of time often degrade or erase critical evidence, making it harder to corroborate allegations. Repeated attacks on the same locations can further complicate efforts to document and verify atrocities.

To mitigate these challenges, investigators rely heavily on technology, such as satellite imagery, drone footage, and geolocation tools, as well as collaborations with humanitarian organizations and local authorities. While these tools enhance evidence collection, they cannot fully capture the scope of atrocities or replace the need for direct investigations.

Political Implications of Holding a Major Power Accountable

Prosecuting a major power like Russia introduces significant political complexities that extend beyond legal and practical considerations. These include:

Geopolitical Ramifications: Holding Russia accountable risks escalating tensions with its allies and destabilizing the broader geopolitical landscape.

Nations reliant on Russia for economic or strategic partnerships may resist supporting international justice efforts, creating a fragmented response.

Selective Justice Perception: Prosecuting Russia while similar crimes in other conflicts remain unaddressed could reinforce accusations of selective justice, undermining the credibility of international mechanisms and fueling cynicism about global accountability systems.

Impact on Peace Negotiations: Pursuing war crimes charges against Russian officials during the conflict could hinder peace talks, as accused individuals may be unwilling to engage in negotiations that could lead to their prosecution. This creates a delicate balance between pursuing justice and fostering diplomatic resolutions to the conflict.

These political considerations underscore the complexity of pursuing justice during an active conflict involving a major power, requiring careful navigation to avoid unintended consequences.

In summary, prosecuting war crimes during the Russia-Ukraine conflict presents immense challenges, from navigating diplomatic and legal barriers to addressing the practical difficulties of evidence collection and witness protection. The political ramifications of holding a powerful state accountable further complicate these efforts, highlighting the need for innovative strategies and sustained international collaboration. This case illustrates the fragility of global justice mechanisms and the urgent need for reforms to enhance their effectiveness in addressing complex, ongoing conflicts. As this chapter concludes, it transitions into exploring the broader implications of this case for global justice, offering lessons that can guide accountability efforts in future conflicts.

4.5 The Broader Implications for Global Justice

The Russia-Ukraine conflict stands as a defining moment for international law and global accountability. As one of the most closely observed conflicts in modern history, it has tested the resilience of international legal frameworks and the ability of institutions like the **International Criminal Court (ICC)** and the **United Nations (UN)** to address war crimes in real time. This section explores what this case reveals about the effectiveness of international law, the lessons it offers for future accountability efforts, and how it reshapes global perceptions of key justice institutions.

What the Russia-Ukraine Case Reveals About the Effectiveness of International Law

The international response to the allegations of war crimes in the Russia-Ukraine conflict underscores both the strengths and limitations of international law.

Strengths: The swift actions taken by the ICC, UN investigative bodies, and independent organizations demonstrate the adaptability of international mechanisms in responding to crises. The deployment of modern technology, such as satellite imagery and AI-based analysis, alongside cross-border collaborations, reflects the evolution of global accountability efforts.

Limitations: The conflict exposes significant gaps in enforcement. Russia's refusal to recognize ICC jurisdiction and its veto power on the UN Security Council highlight the difficulty of prosecuting major powers. These obstacles question the ability of international law to hold influential nations accountable, emphasizing the imbalance in global justice mechanisms.

Additionally, the case reveals the inherent tension between the urgency required in real-time investigations and the thoroughness needed for successful prosecutions. While rapid documentation is vital for preserving evidence, meeting the rigorous legal standards necessary for trials during an active conflict remains a persistent challenge.

Lessons Learned for Future Conflicts and Accountability Efforts

The Russia-Ukraine war offers critical lessons for strengthening global accountability mechanisms in future conflicts:

Strengthening Real-Time Investigations: The conflict underscores the importance of timely and accurate documentation. Expanding the use of satellite imagery, open-source intelligence, and AI-driven analysis can enhance evidence collection and verification in real time, ensuring that critical data is preserved.

Empowering Regional Mechanisms: Regional courts and coalitions, such as the **Joint Investigation Team (JIT)** in Europe, have proven instrumental in supporting accountability efforts. Strengthening these mechanisms can complement global institutions, address jurisdictional gaps, and provide localized solutions.

Reforming Global Institutions: The limitations of the ICC and UN responses emphasize the need for institutional reforms. Enhancing independence, reducing reliance on state cooperation, and addressing perceptions of bias are vital for restoring credibility and ensuring the universality of global justice.

Balancing Justice and Diplomacy: Pursuing justice during active conflicts requires careful integration with peace processes. Developing strategies that align accountability with diplomatic negotiations can help ensure that both justice and stability are achieved, avoiding scenarios where one undermines the other.

How This Case Influences the Global Perception of Institutions Like the ICC and UN

The Russia-Ukraine conflict has placed the ICC, UN, and other global institutions under intense scrutiny, shaping global perceptions of their effectiveness and impartiality.

Perceptions of Selective Justice: The intense focus on Russia has drawn comparisons to conflicts in regions like Yemen, Syria, or the Sahel, where similar atrocities have not received equivalent international attention. This perception of selective justice undermines the universality of global accountability and risks alienating nations in the Global South.

Credibility and Trust: The inability to enforce accountability against a major power has exposed the fragility of international mechanisms. To restore credibility, meaningful reforms are needed, including a more inclusive approach to justice and consistent application of international law across all conflicts.

Opportunities for Renewal: Despite criticism, the heightened focus on institutions like the ICC and UN offers an opportunity for introspection and renewal. By addressing their structural shortcomings, these bodies can emerge stronger, more resilient, and better equipped to address future challenges in an increasingly complex geopolitical landscape.

Thus, the Russia-Ukraine conflict serves as a crucial case study in the pursuit of global justice, revealing both the potential and the limitations of international law. It highlights the need for timely, inclusive, and effective accountability mechanisms while offering valuable lessons for addressing future conflicts. As this chapter concludes, it emphasizes the broader implications of this case for the global justice system, underscoring the urgent need for reform, innovation, and a renewed commitment to fairness and accountability in a polarized world.

Conclusion

The Russia-Ukraine conflict serves as a pivotal case study in the pursuit of accountability during an active war. It exposes both the strengths and vulnerabilities of global justice mechanisms, from the adaptability of institutions like the ICC and UN to the limitations posed by geopolitical dynamics and enforcement challenges. While technological advancements and international collaboration have enhanced documentation and advocacy efforts, the conflict underscores the urgent need for institutional reforms to address jurisdictional gaps and perceptions of selective justice.

This chapter illustrates that achieving accountability during a conflict involving a major power requires innovative approaches and a sustained commitment to impartiality and fairness. The lessons learned from the Russia-Ukraine case offer valuable insights for future conflicts, emphasizing the importance of timely action, regional collaboration, and a balanced integration of justice and diplomacy. As the global community grapples with the complexities of modern warfare, this case underscores the necessity of strengthening international law to ensure that justice remains an attainable goal, even in the most challenging circumstances.

5. The Power of Media and Civil Society

In the quest for accountability and justice, media and civil society serve as powerful catalysts, bridging the gap between documentation and action. Investigative journalism uncovers hidden truths, bringing global attention to atrocities that might otherwise remain obscured. Meanwhile, the rise of social media has transformed conflict documentation, empowering individuals to share real-time accounts of human rights violations. Civil society movements, driven by grassroots activism and international advocacy, amplify these voices, pressuring governments and institutions to act. This chapter explores how media and civil society intersect with global justice mechanisms, highlighting their critical role in exposing atrocities, advocating for accountability, and strengthening the pursuit of justice in an increasingly interconnected world.

5.1 Bridging the Gap: From Documentation to Advocacy

The pursuit of justice in modern conflicts demands a collaborative approach, combining the structured frameworks of international institutions with the dynamic efforts of media and civil society. While global bodies like the **International Criminal Court** (ICC) and the **United Nations** (UN) play pivotal roles in investigating and prosecuting war crimes, their effectiveness is often amplified and supported by independent initiatives. Media and civil society bridge the gap between documentation and advocacy, transforming raw evidence into compelling narratives that galvanize public opinion, influence policy, and drive legal action. Together, they form an indispensable alliance in the fight against impunity.

Connecting Media and Civil Society to Accountability Frameworks

The accountability frameworks explored in earlier chapters—such as the ICC, regional courts, and UN investigative bodies—rely heavily on accurate and comprehensive documentation to build cases against perpetrators. However, these institutions face significant limitations, including:

Geopolitical Dynamics: Major powers often obstruct international investigations, leaving critical evidence overlooked.

Jurisdictional Constraints: Institutional mandates may limit their reach, especially in non-member states or regions of limited cooperation.

Resource Limitations: Many international bodies lack the financial and human resources to investigate all allegations thoroughly.

This is where media and civil society play a transformative role:

Investigative Journalism: Journalists uncover hidden atrocities, providing critical leads and evidence to support institutional investigations. For example, reports from Syria, Myanmar, and Ukraine have offered invaluable insights into violations of international law, shaping global narratives and informing policy decisions.

Civil Society Organizations: Grassroots activists and advocacy groups serve as conduits between affected communities and international institutions. By documenting human rights abuses, gathering testimonies, and organizing advocacy campaigns, they ensure that local realities are represented in global justice efforts.

These contributions not only fill gaps but also enhance the overall effectiveness of international accountability mechanisms.

How Independent Investigations Complement Institutional Justice

Media and civil society's independent investigations complement institutional justice mechanisms in several key ways:

Filling Resource Gaps: International bodies often lack the capacity to investigate extensively in conflict zones. Journalists and NGOs, with their local presence and networks, gather vital information and evidence that might otherwise go undocumented.

Providing Context and Nuance: Institutional investigations are often restricted by legal protocols, which can limit their scope. Media and civil society efforts offer broader perspectives, capturing the human stories behind the data and reports. This emotional and contextual depth enhances public understanding and strengthens the moral imperative for justice.

Building Public Pressure: By disseminating their findings through news outlets, social media, and public campaigns, media and civil society organizations amplify awareness and mobilize public opinion. This pressure can compel governments and international institutions to prioritize accountability efforts and act decisively.

Ensuring Transparency: Independent investigations serve as checks and balances on both perpetrators and institutional bodies. By exposing inaction, bias, or gaps in institutional processes, they ensure that global justice mechanisms remain transparent and credible.

The Russia-Ukraine Conflict: A Case in Point

The Russia-Ukraine war provides a striking example of how media and civil society bridge the gap between documentation and advocacy. Investigative journalists have exposed atrocities such as the Bucha massacres and the targeted bombing of civilian infrastructure, offering critical evidence for international investigations. Through detailed reporting and real-time documentation, they have brought the realities of the conflict to the world's attention.

Civil society organizations, including local activists and international NGOs, have worked tirelessly to document these violations, preserve evidence, and advocate for justice. Collaborations between Ukrainian grassroots movements and global advocacy groups have not only amplified victims' voices but also bolstered efforts by the ICC and UN investigative bodies to build strong cases.

These partnerships exemplify the synergy between independent efforts and institutional frameworks. By working together, media, civil society, and international bodies create a robust accountability ecosystem that ensures evidence is preserved, voices are heard, and justice is pursued.

Thus, media and civil society play a critical role in bridging the gap between documentation and advocacy, ensuring that evidence of atrocities is not only preserved but also acted upon. Their efforts complement the work of institutional mechanisms by bringing visibility, urgency, and depth to the pursuit of justice. As the chapter progresses, we will delve deeper into the specific contributions of investigative journalism, social media, and grassroots movements, exploring how these forces shape accountability and uphold the principles of humanity in the face of conflict.

5.2 Investigative Journalism: Exposing the Truth

Investigative journalism is a cornerstone of accountability, serving as a powerful force in uncovering hidden atrocities and bringing them to the forefront of global attention. In conflict zones, where chaos often obscures the truth, journalists act as witnesses and chroniclers, documenting violations that might otherwise remain invisible. By exposing these truths, investigative journalism shapes global narratives, informs international justice mechanisms, and mobilizes public opinion to demand action. This section delves into the critical role journalists play in conflict settings, notable cases where their work has driven accountability, and the immense challenges they face while operating on the frontlines.

The Role of Journalists in Uncovering Hidden Atrocities

Journalists serve as the eyes and ears of the global community, offering a window into the human suffering and atrocities that occur far from public view. Their work involves several key contributions:

Documenting Evidence: Through photographs, videos, and written accounts, journalists capture evidence of war crimes, human rights abuses, and violations of international law. This documentation often serves as the foundation for legal cases brought before international courts and tribunals.

Amplifying Victims' Voices: By telling the stories of survivors, journalists humanize the statistics of war, ensuring that the voices of those affected are heard. These narratives draw global attention to individual experiences of suffering and resilience, fostering empathy and urgency for action.

Holding Power to Account: Investigative journalism shines a light on the actions of governments, military forces, and non-state actors, exposing their roles in perpetuating or enabling atrocities. This scrutiny pressures those in power to answer for their actions, challenging impunity and reinforcing the principles of justice.

In the Russia-Ukraine war, journalists have been instrumental in documenting events such as the bombing of civilian infrastructure, forced deportations, and mass killings. Their work has provided critical evidence for international investigations and shaped public understanding of the conflict's scale and severity.

Notable Examples of Investigative Journalism Shaping Global Accountability

Throughout history, investigative journalism has been a driving force behind global accountability and justice. Several notable examples illustrate its impact:

The My Lai Massacre (Vietnam War): Seymour Hersh's groundbreaking reporting on the massacre of hundreds of Vietnamese civilians by U.S. soldiers brought global condemnation and led to court-martial proceedings. His work remains a benchmark for holding military actions accountable.

The Bosnian Genocide: Journalists reporting on the Srebrenica massacre provided critical evidence that informed international tribunals. Their detailed accounts helped establish the scale of the atrocities and the culpability of key figures, paving the way for justice in the aftermath of the genocide.

The Russia-Ukraine War: In the ongoing conflict, journalists have exposed atrocities such as the Bucha massacres, providing detailed accounts of civilian executions and mass graves. These reports have been integral to the work of the ICC and other investigative bodies, demonstrating the continued relevance of journalism in conflict zones.

These cases underscore the power of investigative journalism to uncover hidden truths, preserve evidence, and drive accountability efforts at both national and international levels.

Challenges Faced by Journalists in Conflict Zones

The pursuit of truth in war zones comes at a great personal cost for journalists, who often operate under extreme conditions to report on atrocities. Key challenges include:

Physical Danger: Conflict zones are inherently perilous, with journalists frequently exposed to gunfire, bombings, and other forms of violence. Many have lost their lives in the line of duty, underscoring the high stakes of their work.

Intimidation and Retaliation: Journalists reporting on human rights abuses often face threats, harassment, and retaliation from governments, militias, or other actors seeking to suppress their findings. These pressures can jeopardize both their work and their safety.

Access Restrictions: Governments and military forces may restrict access to conflict zones, making it difficult for journalists to gather firsthand evidence or verify reports. These restrictions often limit the scope and depth of their investigations.

Psychological Toll: Witnessing and reporting on atrocities takes a severe emotional toll, with many journalists experiencing trauma or burnout as a result of their work. Despite these challenges, their resilience ensures that critical stories are told.

In summary, investigative journalism remains a vital force in the pursuit of global justice, shedding light on hidden atrocities and holding perpetrators accountable. Through their dedication, journalists not only document violations but also amplify the voices of victims, mobilize public opinion, and provide critical evidence for international investigations. As this chapter progresses, we will explore how the rise of social media has further transformed conflict documentation, empowering individuals to join journalists in exposing the truth and advocating for justice.

5.3 The Rise of Social Media in Documenting Conflict

The advent of social media has revolutionized conflict documentation, offering real-time reporting and empowering individuals to share their experiences directly with a global audience. In modern conflicts, where traditional journalism may be restricted or slow, social media provides a vital platform for capturing and disseminating evidence of atrocities. This section explores how social media has transformed conflict documentation, the rise of citizen journalism in raising global awareness, and the challenges of verifying information in an environment rife with misinformation and disinformation.

Social Media as a Real-Time Documentation Tool in Modern Conflicts

Social media platforms like **Twitter**, **Facebook**, **Instagram**, and **TikTok** have become indispensable tools for documenting conflicts in real time. They allow individuals in conflict zones to bypass traditional media channels and directly share their stories, offering unique advantages:

Speed and Accessibility: Information can be disseminated instantaneously, enabling global audiences to witness events as they unfold.

Unfiltered Content: Social media provides raw and authentic insights into the realities of war, unmediated by editorial filters or institutional gatekeeping.

Decentralized Reporting: A multitude of voices contribute to the narrative, ensuring diverse perspectives and amplifying marginalized experiences.

During the Russia-Ukraine war, social media has played a critical role in documenting the destruction of civilian infrastructure, forced deportations, and mass casualties. Videos captured by residents and shared online have provided compelling evidence for international investigations and have shaped global public opinion. These accounts often complement traditional investigative efforts, bridging gaps in coverage and offering a real-time understanding of the conflict's human impact.

Citizen Journalism and Its Impact on Global Awareness

Social media has given rise to citizen journalism, where ordinary individuals armed with smartphones and social media accounts become frontline reporters. Citizen journalism contributes significantly to conflict documentation by:

Amplifying Marginalized Voices: Social media empowers individuals in remote or underreported areas to share their stories, ensuring their experiences are not overlooked.

Mobilizing Global Action: The immediacy and emotional resonance of citizen-generated content often galvanize international responses, ranging from humanitarian aid to advocacy campaigns.

Supporting Legal Investigations: Videos, photos, and geotagged posts shared by citizens frequently serve as critical evidence for international investigations and prosecutions.

However, the lack of editorial oversight and standardization in citizen journalism raises concerns about accuracy and reliability. While these accounts are invaluable, they require verification to ensure their credibility in legal or institutional contexts.

Verification Challenges: Combating Misinformation and Disinformation

While social media provides unparalleled opportunities for conflict documentation, it also presents significant challenges in ensuring the credibility of shared information. **Misinformation** (false information shared without intent to deceive) and **disinformation** (deliberately false content) proliferate on social platforms, complicating efforts to distinguish fact from fabrication. Key challenges include:

✓ **Manipulated Content:** Videos and images can be edited or taken out of context to mislead audiences, undermining genuine reports.

✓ **Overwhelming Volume:** The sheer quantity of content shared during conflicts makes it difficult for investigators and audiences to verify information efficiently.

✓ **Weaponization of Social Media:** State and non-state actors exploit social media to spread propaganda, sow confusion, and discredit legitimate documentation efforts.

To address these challenges, organizations and platforms employ advanced verification techniques, such as:

✓ **Metadata Analysis:** Examining geotags, timestamps, and digital traces to authenticate content.

✓ **Reverse Image Searches:** Identifying whether images or videos have been previously published or manipulated.

✓ **Crowdsourced Verification:** Engaging experts and online communities to validate content through collaborative efforts.

For example, platforms like **Bellingcat** have pioneered open-source intelligence (OSINT) techniques, using publicly available data to verify and contextualize social media content in conflicts like Syria and Ukraine. These initiatives highlight the potential of technology to counter misinformation while preserving the integrity of conflict documentation.

In summary, social media has transformed the landscape of conflict documentation, empowering individuals to share real-time accounts of war and amplifying the reach of investigative efforts. It bridges the gap between traditional journalism and grassroots reporting, bringing unprecedented visibility to atrocities and mobilizing global responses. However, the challenges of misinformation and disinformation underscore the need for robust verification mechanisms to ensure the credibility of these efforts. As this chapter continues, we will explore how civil society movements harness the power of media, including social platforms, to advocate for accountability and amplify the voices of victims in the pursuit of justice.

5.4 Civil Society Movements: Advocating for Accountability

Civil society movements are at the forefront of global accountability efforts, serving as powerful advocates for justice and amplifying the voices of victims. From grassroots activism to international advocacy campaigns, these movements work tirelessly to ensure that human rights violations are neither ignored nor forgotten. By collaborating with media and legal institutions, civil society bridges the gap between affected communities and global justice mechanisms, driving meaningful change through awareness, pressure, and action. This section explores how grassroots efforts amplify victims' voices, the influence of international campaigns on justice, and the essential synergy between civil society, media, and legal systems.

Grassroots Activism and Its Role in Amplifying Victims' Voices

At the heart of civil society's efforts is grassroots activism, which directly engages with affected communities to document experiences, advocate for justice, and demand accountability. Grassroots activists play a crucial role in ensuring that victims' stories are heard and preserved for posterity. Their contributions include:

Documenting and Preserving Testimonies: Activists collect firsthand accounts from survivors, ensuring that their experiences are not forgotten and can be used as evidence in legal and advocacy efforts.

Mobilizing Local Communities: Through protests, rallies, and awareness campaigns, grassroots movements draw attention to violations and foster solidarity within affected regions.

Advocating for Policy Changes: By pushing for reforms and justice at the national level, local activists lay the groundwork for broader international action, ensuring that victims' needs and perspectives are represented.

In conflicts such as the Russia-Ukraine war, grassroots activists have been instrumental in documenting war crimes, highlighting the plight of displaced civilians, and advocating for international intervention. Their efforts ensure that those directly impacted by atrocities remain central to global justice initiatives.

The Impact of International Advocacy Campaigns on Justice Mechanisms

International advocacy campaigns amplify grassroots efforts by leveraging global platforms to raise awareness, mobilize resources, and influence policymakers. These campaigns often involve coalitions of NGOs, human rights organizations, and activists working in unison to achieve shared goals. Key impacts of these campaigns include:

Raising Awareness: Global campaigns utilize media, public events, and online platforms to spotlight atrocities and ensure they remain in the public eye. For example, initiatives like **#JusticeForUkraine** have successfully rallied international support for accountability efforts during the Russia-Ukraine conflict.

Pressuring Governments and Institutions: Advocacy campaigns mobilize public opinion, compelling governments, international bodies, and corporations to take concrete actions, such as imposing sanctions, launching investigations, or providing humanitarian aid.

Supporting Legal Efforts: Advocacy groups collaborate with legal teams to gather evidence, assist witnesses, and push for the initiation of trials in international courts. Their efforts strengthen the legal foundation for holding perpetrators accountable.

The success of these campaigns lies in their ability to connect local realities with global audiences, transforming individual stories into collective movements that demand systemic change.

Collaborations Between Civil Society, Media, and Legal Institutions

The collaboration between civil society, media, and legal institutions is essential for creating a comprehensive and effective accountability ecosystem. Each entity brings unique strengths to the table, and their synergy enhances the overall impact of justice efforts.

Civil Society and Media: Activists rely on journalists to amplify their findings and share victims' stories with broader audiences. Media coverage provides visibility, ensuring that critical issues are not overlooked and remain at the forefront of public discourse.

Civil Society and Legal Institutions: NGOs and activists provide critical evidence, contextual insights, and connections to affected communities, which strengthen legal investigations. Their work complements institutions like the ICC, addressing gaps in access and documentation.

Media and Legal Institutions: Investigative journalism often uncovers leads that inform legal cases, while media coverage of trials and investigations fosters transparency and public trust in justice mechanisms.

An example of this collaboration is the **Joint Investigation Team (JIT)** working on the Russia-Ukraine war. This initiative brings together NGOs, journalists, and legal experts to share information and build strong cases for accountability. Such integrated approaches ensure that no aspect of justice—documentation, advocacy, or prosecution—is overlooked.

In short, civil society movements are indispensable in advocating for accountability, amplifying the voices of victims, and bridging the gap between local realities and global justice. Through grassroots activism, international advocacy campaigns, and collaborations with media and legal institutions, these movements drive systemic change and uphold the principles of humanity. As this chapter concludes, attention shifts to the broader implications of these efforts, exploring how media and civil society can continue to shape the future of global accountability in an increasingly interconnected world.

5.5 The Synergy Between Media, Civil Society, and Justice

The pursuit of justice in modern conflicts is not the sole responsibility of legal institutions; it is a collective endeavor that relies on the complementary efforts of media, civil society, and international justice mechanisms. Together, these entities create a robust ecosystem where truth is uncovered, voices are amplified, and accountability is pursued. The synergy between media and civil society strengthens the reach and effectiveness of international legal responses, bridging gaps and addressing challenges that institutions alone cannot overcome. This section explores how these efforts converge, lessons from the Russia-Ukraine conflict, and their implications for future global accountability.

How Media and Civil Society Strengthen International Legal Responses

Media and civil society play indispensable roles in enhancing the impact of international legal mechanisms. Their contributions go beyond documentation, providing the visibility, context, and public engagement needed to ensure justice efforts are meaningful and effective. Key contributions include:

Raising Awareness and Mobilizing Action: Media coverage and advocacy campaigns bring attention to atrocities, ensuring they remain global priorities. This visibility generates public pressure on governments and institutions to act decisively, as seen in the international responses to the Russia-Ukraine conflict.

Providing Evidence and Context: Journalists and activists often document evidence and provide nuanced perspectives that complement institutional investigations. Grassroots efforts uncover local stories that inform broader legal cases, adding depth and authenticity to accountability efforts.

Fostering Trust and Transparency: Media coverage of legal proceedings, such as trials at the ICC, demystifies justice processes and builds public confidence in global accountability mechanisms. Transparent reporting ensures that justice is not only done but is seen to be done, reinforcing the legitimacy of international institutions.

In the Russia-Ukraine conflict, investigative journalism and grassroots activism have provided critical evidence that supports the work of international bodies like the ICC and UN. Collaborations between these entities have enhanced the credibility and effectiveness of accountability mechanisms, demonstrating the power of coordinated action.

Lessons from the Russia-Ukraine Conflict for Future Collaboration

The Russia-Ukraine war provides valuable insights into how media and civil society can enhance global justice efforts. Key lessons include:

Real-Time Documentation: Social media and citizen journalism have proven their potential to document atrocities in real time, preserving evidence and raising awareness. Future conflicts can benefit from strengthening these channels while addressing challenges such as misinformation and disinformation.

Collaborative Networks: Partnerships between NGOs, journalists, and international institutions are essential for building comprehensive cases. Expanding these networks can ensure that evidence is thorough, credible, and actionable, bridging gaps in institutional investigations.

Leveraging Technology: The conflict highlights the transformative role of technology, from satellite imagery to AI-driven analysis, in uncovering and verifying atrocities. Investing in these tools can enhance the capacity of media and civil society to contribute effectively to justice efforts.

Balancing Advocacy and Objectivity: Advocacy campaigns must balance mobilizing public opinion with maintaining the impartiality required for legal proceedings. This balance is critical for sustaining trust in both media and justice mechanisms, ensuring that accountability efforts remain credible and effective.

Thus, the synergy between media, civil society, and justice mechanisms underscores the collective nature of global accountability efforts. By raising awareness, providing evidence, and fostering transparency, media and civil society strengthen the capacity of international institutions to address the complexities of modern conflicts. The lessons from the Russia-Ukraine conflict highlight the need for real-time documentation, collaborative networks, and technological advancements to enhance these efforts.

As the chapter concludes, it emphasizes the importance of sustained collaboration between these entities to build a more inclusive and effective global justice system. This synergy not only ensures that the voices of victims are heard but also reinforces the principles of accountability and fairness, paving the way for a more just and equitable world.

Conclusion

This chapter highlights the indispensable role of media and civil society in advancing global accountability. Investigative journalism, social media, and grassroots activism collectively bridge the gap between documentation and action, amplifying the voices of victims and pressuring institutions to pursue justice. Their synergy with international legal mechanisms ensures that evidence is preserved, narratives are shaped, and perpetrators are held accountable.

The Russia-Ukraine conflict underscores the transformative power of these efforts, offering valuable lessons on the importance of real-time documentation, technological innovation, and collaborative networks. Moving forward, strengthening these partnerships and addressing challenges like misinformation and disinformation will be critical to sustaining trust in global accountability systems.

As the book progresses, attention shifts to exploring how these synergistic efforts can be institutionalized and scaled, ensuring that justice remains an attainable and universal goal in an increasingly interconnected world.

6. Lessons from the Past: Case Studies in War Crimes Justice

The pursuit of justice for war crimes is deeply rooted in historical precedents, each offering valuable lessons for addressing modern conflicts. From the Nuremberg Trials that established individual accountability for state-led atrocities, to the groundbreaking work of the tribunals for Yugoslavia and Rwanda, these case studies provide critical insights into the mechanisms, challenges, and successes of international justice. As the Russia-Ukraine war unfolds, these historical experiences offer a roadmap for navigating the complexities of accountability in an interconnected and politically charged world. This chapter explores the key lessons from past tribunals, draws parallels and contrasts with the current conflict, and examines how these precedents continue to shape today's pursuit of justice.

6.1 Nuremberg Trials: The Birth of Modern Accountability

The Nuremberg Trials stand as a pivotal moment in the history of international justice, marking the first time individuals, rather than states, were held accountable for crimes committed during war. Conducted in the aftermath of World War II, these trials established the foundation for modern concepts of war crimes, crimes against humanity, and genocide. They also set critical legal and moral precedents that continue to influence the pursuit of justice in conflicts today.

Origins and Significance of the Nuremberg Trials

The Nuremberg Trials were conceived as a response to the unparalleled atrocities committed by Nazi Germany during World War II. The Holocaust, with the systematic extermination of millions of Jews, Romani people, and other marginalized groups, along with the targeting of civilians and the use of forced labor camps, revealed the depths of human cruelty and underscored the urgent need for accountability.

The Allied powers—comprising the United States, the Soviet Union, the United Kingdom, and France—recognized that traditional methods of justice, such as military tribunals or reparations, were inadequate for addressing crimes of such magnitude. They sought an unprecedented approach: the establishment of an international tribunal to prosecute those most responsible for orchestrating these atrocities.

Held between 1945 and 1946 in Nuremberg, Germany—a city symbolic as a former center of Nazi propaganda—the trials brought 24 prominent Nazi leaders to justice. The location was also chosen for its intact courthouse and prison facilities. The trials were groundbreaking in establishing an international tribunal, with judges and prosecutors from the Allied nations, representing a collective commitment to upholding justice in the aftermath of immense global destruction.

The significance of the Nuremberg Trials extended far beyond the courtroom. They set a global precedent for holding individuals accountable for actions sanctioned by the state, reinforcing the principle that no one, regardless of rank or position, is above the law.

Establishing Individual Accountability for State-Led Atrocities

One of the most revolutionary aspects of the Nuremberg Trials was their rejection of the notion that individuals could escape accountability by claiming they were merely following orders or acting on behalf of a sovereign state. This principle of individual responsibility transformed the landscape of wartime justice, asserting that those who commit or orchestrate atrocities bear personal culpability.

Key principles established at Nuremberg included:

Crimes Against Humanity: Acts such as mass murder, enslavement, and persecution were codified as crimes transcending national boundaries, necessitating international intervention.

War Crimes: Violations of the laws of war, including the targeting of civilians and the mistreatment of prisoners, were formally defined and prosecuted.

Rejection of the "Superior Orders" Defense: The trials firmly established that following orders is not a valid defense for committing atrocities, placing moral and legal responsibility on individuals.

These principles formed the backbone of modern international humanitarian law and have since influenced subsequent legal frameworks and tribunals.

Key Outcomes and Their Enduring Influence on International Law

The Nuremberg Trials concluded with the conviction of 19 defendants, including 12 death sentences, three acquittals, and others receiving varying prison terms. Beyond these verdicts, the trials left an enduring legacy that shaped international law and accountability mechanisms:

Foundation for Future Tribunals: The principles and procedures developed at Nuremberg paved the way for ad hoc tribunals, such as those for Yugoslavia and Rwanda, and for the establishment of the International Criminal Court (ICC) as a permanent mechanism for prosecuting war crimes.

Codification of Legal Principles: The principles articulated at Nuremberg were later enshrined in foundational international treaties, including the **Geneva Conventions** and the **Genocide Convention**, creating a universal framework for addressing war crimes and crimes against humanity.

Moral and Legal Precedent: The trials underscored the universal importance of justice, sending a powerful message that atrocities will not go unpunished, regardless of political or military circumstances. They demonstrated the international community's capacity to rise above division and prioritize accountability.

The legacy of the Nuremberg Trials continues to serve as a guiding light for global governance. Their emphasis on individual accountability, justice, and deterrence remains relevant as modern conflicts, such as the Russia-Ukraine war, challenge existing legal frameworks.

In short, the Nuremberg Trials marked the birth of modern accountability, establishing principles that continue to shape international law and justice.

By holding individuals accountable for state-led atrocities, they redefined the parameters of wartime responsibility and set a precedent for addressing crimes against humanity. As this chapter progresses, the focus will shift to subsequent tribunals, examining how the foundations laid at Nuremberg evolved to meet the challenges of new conflicts and contributed to the pursuit of justice in an increasingly interconnected world.

6.2 The Yugoslavia Tribunal: Addressing Crimes in the Balkans

The International Criminal Tribunal for the former Yugoslavia (ICTY) represented a pivotal step in the evolution of international justice, addressing the widespread atrocities that accompanied the violent breakup of Yugoslavia in the 1990s. Established by the United Nations, the tribunal was tasked with prosecuting individuals responsible for ethnic cleansing, mass killings, and systematic sexual violence in the Balkans. Its work set critical precedents for the prosecution of war crimes in regional conflicts, offering valuable insights into the challenges and opportunities of pursuing justice during and after such crises.

The Mandate and Milestones of the ICTY

Established in 1993 by the United Nations Security Council under Resolution 827, the ICTY became the first international war crimes tribunal since the Nuremberg and Tokyo Trials. Its primary mandate was to hold accountable those responsible for serious violations of international humanitarian law committed between 1991 and 2001 in the territory of the former Yugoslavia. The tribunal aimed to ensure justice, deter future crimes, and contribute to reconciliation in the war-torn region.

Over its 24-year tenure, the ICTY indicted 161 individuals, including high-profile figures such as Slobodan Milošević, the former President of Serbia, and Radovan Karadžić, a key leader of the Bosnian Serbs. Notable convictions included that of Ratko Mladić, infamously known as the "Butcher of Bosnia," for his role in the Srebrenica massacre and other crimes. These cases underscored the tribunal's commitment to prosecuting crimes regardless of the perpetrators' rank or political status.

By the time it concluded operations in 2017, the ICTY had not only delivered justice in numerous cases but also created a comprehensive archive of legal documentation that continues to inform global accountability efforts.

Challenges in Prosecuting Crimes During a Fragmented Conflict

The ICTY faced significant obstacles, many of which stemmed from the complexities of prosecuting crimes in a politically volatile and deeply divided region. One of the tribunal's most pressing challenges was political resistance. Local governments and political leaders frequently obstructed investigations and delayed arrests, with some perpetrators remaining at large for years. For instance, Slobodan Milošević was not apprehended until 2001, nearly eight years after the tribunal's establishment.

Accessing evidence and securing witness testimonies also proved difficult. The ongoing conflict and entrenched ethnic divisions created an environment of fear and mistrust, deterring many individuals from testifying. Even when witnesses were willing, ensuring their safety was a constant concern. Additionally, the ICTY's trials were often lengthy and complex, reflecting the scale and intricacy of the crimes being prosecuted. Milošević's trial, for example, lasted over four years but ended without a verdict due to his death in custody.

Perceptions of bias further complicated the tribunal's work. In many parts of the Balkans, particularly in communities aligned with the accused, the ICTY was viewed as partial or politically motivated. This skepticism hindered its ability to foster reconciliation and build trust among affected populations.

Lessons for Addressing Modern Regional Conflicts

The ICTY's experiences offer several valuable lessons for addressing modern conflicts like the Russia-Ukraine war, where regional dynamics and geopolitical complexities create significant challenges for accountability:

The Importance of a Strong International Mandate: The ICTY's legitimacy stemmed from its UN-backed mandate, underscoring the need for robust international support to secure cooperation from states and local actors.

Balancing Justice with Local Contexts: While the ICTY focused on enforcing international law, integrating local perspectives could have enhanced its reconciliation efforts. Future tribunals should consider combining global principles with culturally sensitive approaches to address community grievances effectively.

Streamlining Judicial Processes: The lengthy trials of the ICTY highlighted the need for efficient judicial processes to deliver timely justice. Modern tribunals can leverage advances in technology and evidence management to streamline proceedings without compromising fairness.

Leveraging Technology for Evidence Collection: Unlike during the ICTY's era, contemporary conflicts benefit from tools such as satellite imagery, digital forensics, and open-source intelligence. These technologies can overcome access challenges and strengthen the evidentiary foundation of cases.

Sustained Commitment to Accountability: The ICTY demonstrated the importance of perseverance in the face of political resistance and logistical hurdles. Ensuring sustained international efforts is critical for delivering justice and deterring future crimes.

In summary, the ICTY illustrated both the potential and the limitations of international justice in addressing atrocities during a fragmented conflict. Its achievements in holding high-profile perpetrators accountable, alongside its struggles with political resistance and local skepticism, provide a framework for tackling modern conflicts like the Russia-Ukraine war. As this chapter continues, attention turns to the International Criminal Tribunal for Rwanda (ICTR), exploring how it confronted the unique challenges of post-genocide justice while advancing the principles of accountability and reconciliation.

6.3 Rwanda and the ICTR: Justice After Genocide

The International Criminal Tribunal for Rwanda (ICTR) was established in response to one of history's most horrific genocides. In 1994, approximately 800,000 people—primarily from the Tutsi ethnic group—were systematically murdered over a span of just 100 days. The international community's delayed response to this atrocity underscored the urgent need for accountability, reconciliation, and justice. The ICTR emerged as a key mechanism to address the aftermath of the genocide, balancing the pursuit of justice with the need to heal a deeply divided society. Its legacy offers critical lessons for addressing mass atrocities in modern conflicts.

The ICTR: Responding to One of History's Worst Genocides

Established by the United Nations Security Council in 1994 under Resolution 955, the ICTR had a mandate to prosecute individuals responsible for genocide, war crimes, and crimes against humanity committed during the Rwandan genocide. The tribunal focused on ensuring accountability for the architects and enablers of the genocide, delivering justice to victims, and fostering national reconciliation.

The ICTR indicted 93 individuals, securing convictions against high-ranking figures such as Jean Kambanda, Rwanda's former Prime Minister, who became the first head of government to be convicted of genocide. The tribunal's work also expanded the legal understanding of genocide and crimes against humanity, particularly through landmark cases that recognized sexual violence as a deliberate tool of war. By the time it concluded operations in 2015, the ICTR had created a wealth of legal precedents and a comprehensive archive of its proceedings, which continue to inform global accountability efforts.

Balancing Justice and Reconciliation in Post-Conflict Societies

One of the ICTR's most significant challenges was balancing the pursuit of justice with the need for reconciliation in a society fractured by ethnic violence and mistrust. These objectives often came into tension as the tribunal sought to address both the scale of the crimes and the needs of the affected communities.

The ICTR focused primarily on prosecuting high-level perpetrators, while Rwanda's domestic justice system, including community-based **Gacaca courts**, handled lower-level offenders. This dual approach ensured that justice was pursued across the spectrum of responsibility. While the ICTR provided a platform for victims to share their stories and seek accountability, its focus on high-profile cases left many victims feeling excluded. Additionally, the tribunal's location in Arusha, Tanzania, distanced it from the communities most affected by the genocide, limiting its ability to directly foster reconciliation and social cohesion.

The tribunal's work highlighted the challenges of rebuilding trust in post-conflict societies. While its emphasis on accountability sent a powerful message about the consequences of impunity, it also underscored the importance of proximity and accessibility in fostering community engagement and healing.

Insights for Addressing Mass Atrocities in Modern Conflicts

The ICTR's experiences provide valuable lessons for addressing mass atrocities in contemporary conflicts, including those in Ukraine, Syria, and Myanmar. Key insights include:

The Need for Swift Action: The delayed establishment of the ICTR demonstrated the importance of timely intervention to preserve evidence and initiate accountability. Modern conflicts demand mechanisms that can act quickly to address atrocities and prevent further harm.

Integrating Justice and Reconciliation Efforts: Post-conflict societies require a holistic approach that balances justice with reconciliation. The ICTR's collaboration with local Gacaca courts illustrates the value of combining international tribunals with community-based mechanisms to create a more inclusive and culturally sensitive process.

Recognizing the Role of Victims: Victims must be central to accountability efforts. Providing avenues for victim testimony, reparations, and participation in the justice process fosters healing, empowerment, and trust in the system.

Addressing Sexual Violence: The ICTR set a precedent by recognizing sexual violence as a tool of genocide, paving the way for a stronger focus on gender-based crimes in modern accountability frameworks. Expanding and strengthening this focus remains a critical priority.

Locating Justice Near Affected Communities: Proximity plays a vital role in fostering trust and engagement. Modern accountability mechanisms should prioritize accessibility to bridge the gap between global justice efforts and local realities, ensuring that affected communities feel connected to the process.

In conclusion, the ICTR's efforts to address the Rwandan genocide represent a landmark achievement in international justice. Its successes in prosecuting key perpetrators and expanding legal definitions of crimes, alongside its challenges in balancing justice with reconciliation, offer critical lessons for modern accountability efforts. The tribunal's legacy highlights the importance of integrating justice with reconciliation, empowering victims, and fostering community involvement. As the chapter progresses, the focus shifts to examining how historical tribunals, including the ICTR, provide a framework for addressing the challenges of pursuing accountability in contemporary conflicts like the Russia-Ukraine war.

6.4 Parallels and Contrasts with the Russia-Ukraine War

The pursuit of accountability in the Russia-Ukraine war shares significant parallels with historical tribunals such as those established for Nuremberg, Yugoslavia, and Rwanda. However, it is also shaped by distinct challenges and opportunities arising from modern geopolitical dynamics, technological advancements, and the realities of documenting atrocities during an ongoing conflict. Exploring these similarities and differences offers valuable insights into how lessons from the past inform current efforts and how contemporary innovations demand new approaches to justice.

How Lessons from Historical Tribunals Apply to the Current Conflict

The principles and practices established by earlier tribunals remain relevant in guiding accountability efforts in the Russia-Ukraine war. A few critical lessons include:

First, **accountability for leaders and perpetrators** is central to achieving justice. The Nuremberg Trials and the ICTY set the precedent of rejecting the defense of "just following orders," emphasizing individual responsibility. This principle is directly applicable to the Russia-Ukraine war, where international bodies like the ICC are investigating allegations of war crimes and crimes against humanity committed by political and military leaders.

Second, the emphasis on **documentation as the foundation of justice** in tribunals such as the ICTR and ICTY underscores the importance of meticulous evidence collection. These precedents highlight the need for robust documentation in Ukraine, ensuring that evidence of atrocities is preserved and verified for future legal proceedings.

Third, **international collaboration** plays a pivotal role in building strong cases. The collaborative approach of the ICTY is mirrored in the efforts of the

Joint Investigation Team (JIT) for Ukraine, which brings together resources and expertise from multiple nations to ensure comprehensive investigations.

Key Differences in Geopolitical Dynamics, Evidence Collection, and International Responses

While historical tribunals provide a valuable framework, the Russia-Ukraine war presents unique complexities due to its contemporary context:

Geopolitical Dynamics create significant challenges. Unlike Nuremberg and ICTY, which were conducted after the respective conflicts had ended, the Russia-Ukraine war is ongoing. This makes evidence collection and accountability initiatives more challenging, as the global community remains divided on the conflict's resolution. Additionally, Russia's status as a major power with veto authority in the UN Security Council limits international responses, a challenge not faced to the same extent by historical tribunals.

Real-Time Documentation and Evidence Collection differentiate the Russia-Ukraine conflict from historical cases. While evidence for earlier tribunals was often gathered post-conflict, modern technology enables real-time documentation through social media platforms, satellite imagery, and open-source intelligence (OSINT). While these tools provide immediate insights, the sheer volume of data can overwhelm investigators and pose verification challenges.

The **diverse international responses** to the Russia-Ukraine war further complicate global accountability. Historical tribunals like ICTY and ICTR benefited from relatively unified international mandates, often backed by the United Nations. In contrast, responses to the Ukraine conflict are fragmented, with Western nations imposing sanctions and providing military aid while other regions maintain neutral or aligned stances with Russia. This division hinders the establishment of a cohesive justice mechanism.

The Role of Modern Technology in Advancing Accountability Compared to Historical Cases

Modern technology has revolutionized the methods of documenting and investigating war crimes, addressing many challenges faced by historical tribunals while introducing new complexities:

Real-Time Evidence Gathering through tools such as drones, geospatial mapping, and satellite imagery allows investigators to document atrocities as they occur, preserving crucial evidence for building legal cases. These methods offer significant advantages over the limited evidence-collection techniques available during the Nuremberg Trials or ICTY.

The rise of **citizen journalism and social media** has democratized conflict documentation, enabling civilians in war zones to act as real-time witnesses. Platforms like Twitter, TikTok, and YouTube amplify voices from the ground, complementing traditional investigative efforts. However, they also introduce risks of misinformation and disinformation, requiring robust verification processes.

AI and Data Analytics have streamlined evidence verification, helping identify patterns in war crimes and authenticate photo and video metadata. While these tools address challenges that historical tribunals struggled with, such as handling large volumes of evidence, they require careful oversight to ensure ethical use and prevent misuse.

Finally, modern technology has enhanced **global awareness and mobilization.** The immediacy and emotional impact of real-time content shared online have galvanized advocacy efforts and increased pressure on governments and institutions to act. This level of visibility and engagement was not possible during the ICTY or ICTR eras.

In summary, the Russia-Ukraine war presents both opportunities and challenges for accountability efforts, shaped by lessons from historical tribunals and the unique realities of modern conflict. While the principles established by Nuremberg, ICTY, and ICTR remain relevant, contemporary geopolitical dynamics and technological advancements demand innovative approaches to justice. By integrating historical lessons with modern tools and strategies, the global community can strengthen accountability mechanisms and adapt to the complexities of today's warfare. As the chapter concludes, it transitions to examining the broader implications of these parallels and contrasts for shaping the future of global justice systems.

6.5 Historical Precedents Shaping Today's Pursuit of Justice

The pursuit of justice for war crimes has been deeply influenced by historical precedents, from the Nuremberg Trials to the tribunals for Yugoslavia and Rwanda. These milestones laid the groundwork for modern international legal frameworks, underscoring the importance of accountability and the necessity of robust mechanisms to address atrocities. As global conflicts evolve, so too must the frameworks designed to confront them. This section explores the evolution of international law since Nuremberg, the need to adapt past models to contemporary challenges, and how historical lessons can guide the strengthening of global accountability mechanisms.

The Evolution of International Legal Frameworks Since Nuremberg

The Nuremberg Trials marked the inception of modern international justice, establishing principles that have shaped the development of global accountability mechanisms. Key milestones in this evolution include:

The **codification of international law** saw the principles of Nuremberg enshrined in foundational legal instruments, such as the **Geneva Conventions (1949)** and the **Genocide Convention (1948)**. These frameworks defined war crimes, crimes against humanity, and genocide as punishable offenses under international law, setting universal standards for accountability.

The establishment of **ad hoc tribunals** such as the ICTY and ICTR in the 1990s demonstrated the international community's commitment to addressing atrocities in specific regions. These tribunals refined legal standards, including the recognition of sexual violence as a weapon of war, and proved that accountability could be pursued even in complex and politically sensitive contexts.

The creation of the **International Criminal Court (ICC)** in 2002 marked a significant step forward. Established through the **Rome Statute**, the ICC provides a permanent mechanism to prosecute individuals for serious international crimes. Unlike ad hoc tribunals, the ICC's mandate is global and ongoing, representing a shift toward a more unified and comprehensive approach to accountability.

Modern frameworks also increasingly emphasize the **integration of victim participation**, recognizing victims' roles as central to the justice process. This shift reflects lessons learned from earlier tribunals, where victim engagement was often limited, and highlights the importance of inclusivity in achieving meaningful justice.

The Importance of Adapting Past Models to Contemporary Challenges

While historical frameworks provide a solid foundation, modern conflicts present unique challenges that demand innovative approaches:

Complex geopolitical dynamics characterize many contemporary conflicts. Unlike the relatively unified global response during Nuremberg or the ICTR, conflicts such as the Russia-Ukraine war are marked by polarized international relations. Mechanisms for accountability must be designed to function effectively amid such divisions, ensuring impartiality and resilience.

Technological advancements have transformed evidence collection and documentation. The rise of social media, satellite imagery, and AI-driven analysis enables real-time documentation of atrocities but also introduces new complexities, such as managing the sheer scale of data and ensuring its authenticity.

The increasing prevalence of **non-state actors** in conflicts, including terrorist organizations and militias, poses challenges for accountability frameworks originally designed for state-led crimes. Addressing these actors requires adaptations to existing legal models and the development of new mechanisms tailored to their unique dynamics.

Balancing justice with reconciliation remains a critical consideration. Lessons from Rwanda's post-genocide efforts illustrate the need for holistic approaches that integrate legal justice with societal healing, ensuring that accountability efforts contribute to long-term peace and stability.

Building on Historical Lessons to Strengthen Global Accountability Mechanisms

Historical tribunals offer several key lessons for strengthening modern accountability efforts:

The **need for timely action** is evident in the delays seen with the ICTY and ICTR, which highlighted the importance of swift responses to preserve evidence and prevent further atrocities. Modern mechanisms must prioritize speed without compromising thoroughness.

Empowering regional and local mechanisms can ensure a more inclusive and culturally sensitive approach to justice. Combining international frameworks with community-based initiatives, such as Rwanda's Gacaca courts, enables broader participation and addresses local grievances.

Expanding **jurisdiction and international cooperation** is critical. The ICC's challenges in prosecuting crimes committed by non-member states emphasize the need for broader global support and reforms to enhance its reach and effectiveness.

Ensuring inclusivity and representation is vital for fostering trust and legitimacy in justice processes. Accountability efforts must amplify the voices of victims and marginalized groups, ensuring that justice addresses the needs of those most affected.

Leveraging modern technology can enhance the efficiency and transparency of legal proceedings. Tools for documentation, analysis, and evidence presentation address longstanding challenges in international justice, enabling more robust and credible cases.

In summary, the evolution of international justice since Nuremberg reflects humanity's enduring commitment to accountability, even in the face of immense challenges. However, as modern conflicts grow more complex, historical models must be adapted to address new realities. By building on the lessons of the past and embracing innovation, the global community can strengthen accountability mechanisms, ensuring that justice remains a cornerstone of international relations. As this chapter concludes, it sets the stage for exploring future strategies to institutionalize and scale these efforts in the pursuit of a more just and equitable world.

Conclusion

This chapter illustrates the enduring influence of historical tribunals on the evolution of international justice. From the Nuremberg Trials to the ICTY and ICTR, these case studies highlight the principles of accountability, justice, and reconciliation that continue to guide efforts in addressing modern atrocities.

Their successes and limitations provide a valuable framework for tackling contemporary challenges, such as the Russia-Ukraine war, where geopolitical complexities and technological advancements demand innovative approaches.

As the global community navigates these complexities, the integration of historical lessons with modern tools and inclusive practices becomes paramount. Timely action, victim-centered approaches, and the use of advanced technologies are essential for strengthening global accountability mechanisms. The chapter underscores that by building on these precedents and embracing innovation, international justice can adapt to the evolving nature of conflict and remain a cornerstone of global governance.

This chapter sets the stage for exploring strategies to institutionalize and scale these efforts, ensuring that justice remains accessible, equitable, and effective in an increasingly interconnected world.

7. Political and Practical Challenges

The pursuit of global justice is often hindered by the interplay of politics and practicality. While international mechanisms like the ICC and the UN have made significant strides in addressing war crimes and atrocities, their efforts are frequently obstructed by political biases, sovereignty concerns, and enforcement challenges. The gridlock within the United Nations Security Council, the tension between state sovereignty and global accountability, and the complexities of enforcing international rulings against powerful nations underscore the difficulties of translating principles into action. This chapter explores these challenges, examining how geopolitics, institutional structures, and practical realities shape—and sometimes impede—the pursuit of justice in an increasingly polarized world.

7.1 The UN Security Council: Gridlock and Political Biases

The United Nations Security Council (UNSC) is a cornerstone of the global governance system, entrusted with the critical mandate of maintaining international peace and security. It plays a pivotal role in addressing conflicts, sanctioning interventions, and supporting accountability for war crimes and atrocities. However, the structural dynamics and decision-making processes of the Council often undermine its effectiveness. Political biases, the misuse of veto power, and the competing interests of its permanent members frequently lead to gridlock, leaving victims of atrocities without justice and enabling perpetrators to evade accountability. This section examines how the UNSC's structure and politics impede its mandate, with illustrative examples from conflicts like Syria and Ukraine.

The Structure of the UNSC and Its Impact on Accountability

The UNSC wields immense power in global governance, but its structure often limits its ability to act effectively in addressing war crimes and promoting accountability. The Council consists of five permanent members with veto power—the United States, Russia, China, the United Kingdom, and France—and ten rotating members. While this structure was designed to reflect the post-World War II balance of power, it often skews decisions toward the geopolitical interests of its most influential members rather than the collective pursuit of justice.

The veto power granted to the five permanent members is a particularly contentious feature. This mechanism allows any of these nations to block resolutions, even when there is widespread international support. While originally intended to promote stability and prevent unilateral actions, the veto has frequently been misused to shield allies or protect national interests, stalling accountability efforts and weakening the global justice system.

The Role of Veto Power in Stalling Justice Initiatives

The veto's impact is most evident in cases where justice initiatives have been obstructed. During the Syrian civil war, repeated attempts to refer the situation to the International Criminal Court (ICC) were vetoed by Russia and China. These actions effectively shielded the Syrian government from international scrutiny despite overwhelming evidence of atrocities, including chemical weapons attacks and indiscriminate violence against civilians.

Similarly, in the Russia-Ukraine war, Russia's veto power has consistently blocked resolutions addressing its alleged war crimes and aggression. This has paralyzed the Council's ability to act, undermining efforts to ensure accountability. The pattern of veto misuse illustrates the difficulty of pursuing justice when powerful nations directly involved in conflicts wield decisive influence over accountability mechanisms.

Beyond individual conflicts, the misuse of veto power creates a broader environment where political interests take precedence over human rights and accountability. This dynamic fosters a sense of impunity among perpetrators, weakens the credibility of the UNSC, and erodes trust in international institutions as neutral arbiters of justice.

Geopolitical Gridlock: Examples from Syria and Ukraine

The UNSC's gridlock is not an isolated issue but a recurring trend in global conflicts. In Syria, vetoes from Russia and China repeatedly blocked efforts to investigate chemical weapons attacks and other human rights violations. These actions stymied international responses, prolonging the suffering of civilians and delaying justice for victims.

In Ukraine, the situation highlights even starker contradictions. Russia, as a permanent member of the UNSC, has used its veto power to obstruct resolutions addressing its alleged war crimes and aggressive actions. This impasse underscores the inherent flaw in allowing a party to a conflict to have such decisive control over mechanisms meant to ensure accountability. The inability of the UNSC to act decisively in these cases highlights the Council's structural and procedural weaknesses in addressing urgent crises.

The Need for Reform

The structural issues and political biases within the UNSC highlight the urgent need for reform. Limiting the use of the veto in cases involving mass atrocities or crimes against humanity is a critical first step. Proposals such as the **French-Mexican initiative**, which calls for permanent members to voluntarily suspend their veto rights in situations of genocide or large-scale war crimes, aim to address this issue. Additionally, expanding the Council's permanent membership to include a broader range of nations could reduce the dominance of a few powerful states and promote a more inclusive approach to decision-making.

Ensuring that the UNSC prioritizes justice and accountability over geopolitical interests is essential for maintaining its credibility and effectiveness. Structural reforms that balance power more equitably and mechanisms that enhance the Council's responsiveness to global crises are vital for restoring trust in its ability to uphold international law.

Thus, the UNSC's current structure and decision-making processes often impede its ability to fulfill its mandate of maintaining global peace and security.

The misuse of veto power, coupled with geopolitical gridlock, undermines accountability efforts and erodes trust in the international justice system. Addressing these challenges through structural reforms and greater inclusivity is essential for ensuring that justice is not obstructed by the interests of a few powerful states. As this chapter progresses, attention turns to other political and practical challenges, such as the tension between sovereignty and global accountability, that intersect with these systemic issues.

7.2 Sovereignty versus Global Accountability

The tension between state sovereignty and international justice mechanisms lies at the heart of many challenges in the pursuit of global accountability. Sovereignty, a cornerstone of international relations, grants states the right to govern without external interference, ensuring independence in domestic affairs. However, this principle often conflicts with efforts to address war crimes and crimes against humanity, where global oversight becomes necessary to uphold justice. Balancing the sanctity of sovereignty with the imperatives of accountability has proven to be one of the most persistent and complex dilemmas in global justice.

The Tension Between Sovereignty and International Justice Mechanisms

International justice mechanisms, such as the **International Criminal Court (ICC)**, are designed to address atrocities that transcend national boundaries, including genocide, war crimes, and crimes against humanity. These mechanisms operate on the premise that accountability is a universal obligation, yet their mandates frequently clash with the principle of sovereignty, which gives states the authority to handle domestic matters independently.

Governments accused of atrocities often invoke sovereignty to resist international investigations and prosecutions, arguing that external intervention infringes on their jurisdiction. This resistance is particularly acute when governments themselves are implicated in crimes. For example, Sudan's defiance of ICC proceedings against former President **Omar al-Bashir**, who was indicted for crimes committed in Darfur, highlighted how sovereignty can be wielded as a shield against accountability. Similarly, the reluctance of powerful nations like the United States, Russia, and China to ratify the **Rome Statute**, which established the ICC, underscores their intent to protect their sovereignty and avoid external scrutiny.

This conflict reveals the paradox of sovereignty: while it safeguards national independence, it can also enable impunity for crimes that demand international attention.

Historical Resistance to Accountability Efforts and Its Implications

Resistance to international justice is not a new phenomenon. Historically, states have prioritized sovereignty over accountability, often at the expense of victims and global justice. During the **Nuremberg Trials**, critics argued that prosecuting individuals for state-sanctioned crimes violated the principles of sovereignty. Despite these objections, the trials set a precedent for prioritizing accountability over absolute sovereignty in cases of mass atrocities.

In more recent history, the **ICTY** and **ICTR** faced significant resistance from local governments and political leaders. For instance, Serbia initially refused to cooperate with the ICTY, delaying the arrest of high-profile figures like **Slobodan Milošević**. These delays undermined the tribunals' ability to act swiftly and reinforced the perception that international justice mechanisms are ineffective when faced with sovereign resistance.

Such resistance has broader implications. When states refuse to cooperate, they not only impede justice but also erode the credibility of international institutions. This creates a dangerous precedent for impunity, weakening the global framework designed to address atrocities and leaving victims without recourse.

Balancing National Interests with the Need for Global Oversight

Reconciling state sovereignty with global accountability requires innovative and context-sensitive strategies that respect national interests while ensuring justice is not sacrificed.

Complementarity: The ICC's principle of complementarity allows it to intervene only when national judicial systems are unwilling or unable to prosecute crimes. This approach respects sovereignty while ensuring a safety net exists to address egregious violations.

Regional Mechanisms: Strengthening regional justice mechanisms can bridge the gap between national and international efforts. For example, the African Union's initiatives to establish regional courts for crimes under international law demonstrate how regional solutions can address sovereignty concerns while maintaining accountability.

Diplomatic Engagement: Building trust through diplomatic efforts and demonstrating the long-term benefits of accountability for stability and peace can reduce resistance. Diplomatic pressure, coupled with incentives for cooperation, can encourage states to engage with international justice mechanisms.

Balancing Justice and Stability: Prioritizing reconciliation and peacebuilding alongside accountability can address sovereignty concerns. For instance, Rwanda's **Gacaca courts**, which operated in tandem with the ICTR, addressed local grievances in a culturally sensitive manner, blending global principles with community-based approaches.

In summary, the tension between sovereignty and global accountability is a complex and enduring challenge. While sovereignty is vital for maintaining order in international relations, it cannot serve as a pretext for impunity in cases of war crimes and crimes against humanity. By adopting strategies that respect sovereignty while promoting accountability, the international community can create a more balanced and effective approach to justice. As this chapter progresses, attention shifts to enforcement challenges, exploring how geopolitical realities impact the implementation of global justice mechanisms.

7.3 When Justice Meets Geopolitics: Enforcement Issues

The enforcement of international justice frequently encounters significant obstacles, particularly when powerful nations or their allies are involved. While international courts and tribunals play a critical role in delivering justice, their ability to enforce rulings is often undermined by geopolitical realities, alliances, and economic dependencies. These challenges leave victims without recourse and create a perception of impunity for those shielded by global power dynamics. This section examines the difficulties of enforcing international rulings against influential states, explores the role of alliances and economic dependencies in shaping accountability, and highlights key case studies that reveal enforcement gaps, such as the limitations of the International Criminal Court (ICC).

Challenges in Enforcing International Rulings Against Powerful Nations

Enforcing international rulings becomes especially challenging when the accused party is a major global power or enjoys the protection of one. Nations such as the United States, Russia, and China, which are not signatories to the Rome Statute, operate outside the ICC's jurisdiction. Even when international courts issue warrants or rulings, the absence of enforcement mechanisms means these decisions are often ignored. For instance, despite the ICC issuing an arrest warrant for Sudan's former President **Omar al-Bashir** for war crimes in Darfur, he continued to travel freely to countries, including ICC member states, that were either unwilling or unable to execute the warrant. Political considerations and fear of retaliation often outweighed obligations to international law.

In conflicts involving major powers, such as the **Russia-Ukraine war**, enforcement challenges are even more pronounced. Russia's position as a permanent member of the United Nations Security Council (UNSC) grants it significant leverage, including the veto power to block resolutions addressing its actions. This dynamic effectively shields it from meaningful international repercussions, illustrating how geopolitical influence can obstruct justice and accountability.

The Role of Alliances and Economic Dependencies in Shaping Accountability

Global alliances and economic dependencies frequently complicate the enforcement of international justice. Nations aligned with powerful states may resist implementing arrest warrants or supporting accountability measures to protect their strategic or economic interests. For example, countries reliant on Russian energy exports often avoid taking actions that could jeopardize these relationships, even when facing significant international pressure.

Similarly, alliances within blocs such as NATO or regional organizations can shape accountability dynamics. The United States, for instance, has historically used its influence to shield its allies from international scrutiny and has actively opposed ICC investigations involving its personnel. For example, when the ICC sought to investigate alleged war crimes committed by U.S. forces in Afghanistan, the U.S. government imposed sanctions on ICC officials and refused to cooperate. These actions highlight how alliances and economic dependencies can create dual standards in enforcement, undermining the universality of international justice and eroding trust in global mechanisms.

Case Studies Highlighting Enforcement Gaps

Several high-profile cases illustrate the limitations of enforcement mechanisms and the broader challenges facing international justice:

The Omar al-Bashir Case: Despite being indicted by the ICC for war crimes and crimes against humanity in Darfur, Omar al-Bashir traveled to multiple countries, including ICC member states, without being arrested. This failure underscored the lack of political will and practical capacity to enforce rulings against a sitting head of state.

The Russia-Ukraine War: Allegations of war crimes in Ukraine have drawn significant international attention, but Russia's geopolitical influence and veto power in the UNSC have stymied efforts to address these crimes through formal channels. The ICC's inability to enforce rulings against non-signatory states like Russia further highlights its limitations.

The U.S. and ICC Investigations: The ICC's attempts to investigate alleged war crimes committed by U.S. forces in Afghanistan faced strong opposition from the U.S. government, including the imposition of sanctions against ICC officials. This resistance demonstrated the challenges of holding powerful nations accountable and exposed the constraints of international justice mechanisms when confronted with major geopolitical players.

Addressing Enforcement Challenges

Overcoming these enforcement challenges requires innovative approaches and strengthened mechanisms that address the systemic weaknesses of current frameworks:

Building Broader Consensus: Strengthening alliances among states committed to accountability can create a counterbalance to powerful nations that resist enforcement. Collaborative coalitions can amplify pressure and enhance the credibility of international justice efforts.

Empowering Regional Mechanisms: Regional courts and justice systems can complement international mechanisms by addressing crimes within their jurisdiction, particularly when global institutions face resistance. For example, African-led initiatives such as the **African Court on Human and Peoples' Rights** demonstrate the potential of regional solutions.

Leveraging Economic and Diplomatic Pressure: Sanctions, travel bans, and diplomatic isolation can compel compliance with international rulings, even against powerful nations or their allies. These measures, while not foolproof, can create tangible consequences for non-compliance.

Enhancing the ICC's Authority: Expanding the ICC's jurisdiction and improving cooperation frameworks with non-signatory states can address enforcement gaps. Additionally, establishing clearer consequences for non-compliance, such as automatic sanctions, can strengthen the ICC's impact.

Thus, the enforcement of international justice remains one of the most significant challenges in the global accountability framework, particularly when geopolitical interests come into play. The interplay of alliances, economic dependencies, and the influence of powerful nations often undermines the effectiveness of international rulings, leaving victims without justice and perpetrators unaccountable. Addressing these enforcement gaps through innovative strategies and strengthened mechanisms is essential to ensure that justice is guided by principles of accountability and fairness rather than power dynamics. As the chapter progresses, attention turns to exploring strategies for bridging these divides and building a more unified and resilient global justice system.

7.4 Bridging the Divide: Toward a More Unified Global Justice System

The challenges posed by political biases, sovereignty conflicts, and enforcement gaps demand innovative reforms and collaborative strategies to strengthen the global justice system. Bridging the divide between national interests and international accountability requires reimagining existing frameworks to make them more equitable, effective, and resilient. By addressing systemic flaws, integrating modern technologies, and empowering civil society, the global community can work toward a unified justice system capable of responding to the complexities of modern conflicts.

Potential Reforms to Address Political Biases and Strengthen Enforcement

Reforming international justice structures, particularly the United Nations Security Council (UNSC) and the International Criminal Court (ICC), is critical to reducing political biases and improving enforcement mechanisms.

One significant reform involves **limiting the use of veto power** within the UNSC, particularly in cases involving mass atrocities or crimes against humanity. Proposals such as the French-Mexican initiative to restrict veto use in situations of genocide or war crimes aim to ensure that justice is prioritized over geopolitical interests. Additionally, **expanding UNSC permanent membership** to include a more diverse range of nations could reduce the dominance of a few powerful states and promote a more balanced approach to global accountability.

Strengthening the ICC's enforcement mechanisms is another critical area for reform. This includes enhancing cooperation frameworks with non-signatory states and establishing mechanisms for the direct enforcement of arrest warrants through international or regional coalitions. To improve compliance, **clearer consequences for non-cooperation**, such as automatic sanctions or diplomatic restrictions, could serve as a deterrent against obstruction and enhance the ICC's global impact.

Innovative Approaches to Reconciling Sovereignty with Global Accountability

Balancing the principle of state sovereignty with the need for international oversight requires innovative and collaborative approaches that build trust and mutual respect.

The ICC's **principle of complementarity**, which allows the Court to intervene only when national judicial systems fail to act, provides a model for reconciling sovereignty with global accountability. Encouraging states to strengthen their domestic justice systems through technical and financial support can reduce resistance to international mechanisms while ensuring that justice is delivered locally.

The use of **hybrid courts** offers another solution. These courts, such as the Extraordinary Chambers in the Courts of Cambodia, combine international expertise with local participation, allowing for culturally sensitive approaches to accountability while maintaining global standards. Expanding such models can address sovereignty concerns while ensuring effective prosecutions.

Diplomatic initiatives, such as confidence-building measures and **regional partnerships**, can also align national interests with global justice goals. Framing accountability efforts as tools for stability and peace, rather than as external interference, can build trust and encourage reluctant states to engage with international mechanisms.

The Role of Technology and Civil Society in Overcoming Political Obstacles

Technology and civil society have transformative potential to overcome the political and practical challenges that hinder global justice efforts.

Technological advancements, such as **satellite imagery, blockchain for evidence preservation, and artificial intelligence (AI) for data analysis**, provide innovative tools for documenting atrocities and verifying evidence. These technologies enhance the accuracy and credibility of investigations while reducing dependence on state cooperation by enabling independent evidence collection. For instance, open-source intelligence (OSINT) platforms like **Bellingcat** have demonstrated the effectiveness of technology in uncovering war crimes and supporting international investigations.

Civil society organizations and grassroots movements play a vital role in bridging the gap between affected communities and global justice mechanisms. By amplifying victims' voices, raising awareness, and pressuring governments and institutions to act, civil society fosters public trust and accountability. Partnerships between civil society, media, and international institutions further strengthen these efforts, ensuring transparency and reinforcing the principles of fairness and equity in global governance.

In short, bridging the divide between sovereignty and global accountability is crucial for creating a unified and effective justice system. Addressing political biases through structural reforms, embracing innovative approaches such as hybrid courts, and leveraging technology and civil society are essential steps in overcoming the challenges that currently impede international justice. These efforts not only ensure that perpetrators are held accountable but also reinforce the foundational principles of fairness and equity that underpin global governance. Continued collaboration and innovation are imperative to advancing the cause of international justice in an increasingly interconnected and complex world.

As the chapter concludes, it emphasizes that building a resilient global justice system is not only a legal imperative but also a moral responsibility in the pursuit of a more just and equitable future.

Conclusion

This chapter, explores the complex interplay of political biases, sovereignty conflicts, and enforcement challenges that impede global justice. It underscores the structural weaknesses of mechanisms like the UNSC and ICC, highlighting how geopolitical realities and power dynamics often obstruct accountability efforts. However, the chapter also emphasizes pathways for reform, including structural changes to reduce biases, innovative approaches to reconcile sovereignty with accountability, and the transformative potential of technology and civil society.

Bridging the divide between national interests and global oversight requires collaboration, innovation, and sustained commitment. By addressing systemic flaws and empowering both international mechanisms and grassroots initiatives, the global community can strengthen justice frameworks to ensure fairness and equity. The chapter concludes by affirming that building a resilient global justice system is not only a legal imperative but also a moral responsibility, essential for addressing modern conflicts and fostering a more just and equitable world.

8. Restorative Justice: Bridging Accountability and Reconciliation

Justice in the aftermath of conflict is not solely about punishment; it is also about rebuilding societies, fostering healing, and preventing future atrocities. While retributive justice focuses on holding perpetrators accountable, restorative justice emphasizes acknowledgment, dialogue, and the restoration of relationships. Transitional mechanisms such as truth commissions, reparations, and reconciliation initiatives provide an essential bridge between the demands of accountability and the need for societal healing. This chapter explores how restorative justice complements traditional legal frameworks, drawing on global examples to highlight its role in addressing the human and social dimensions of justice. By examining truth-telling, reparations, and reconciliation practices, it underscores the importance of integrating these approaches to achieve sustainable peace in post-conflict societies.

8.1 The Concept of Restorative Justice

Restorative justice offers a transformative approach to addressing the aftermath of conflict, moving beyond the punitive focus of retributive justice. While retributive justice seeks to hold perpetrators accountable through formal legal mechanisms, restorative justice centers on healing, acknowledgment, and the restoration of relationships. It emphasizes the human dimensions of justice, providing a platform for victims, perpetrators, and communities to engage in dialogue, confront truths, and collectively work toward reconciliation.

Moving Beyond Retributive Justice

Retributive justice plays a vital role in ensuring accountability for war crimes, crimes against humanity, and other gross violations of human rights.

However, its focus on punishment often overlooks the broader societal needs that emerge in the aftermath of conflict. Victims may feel alienated from rigid legal processes, while communities struggle to rebuild trust and cohesion. Restorative justice seeks to address these gaps by creating spaces for acknowledgment and dialogue, fostering an environment where all parties can share their experiences and contribute to collective healing.

Restorative justice is not a replacement for retributive systems but a complementary approach. By focusing on the needs of victims and the responsibilities of perpetrators, it aims to repair harm and rebuild relationships, laying the groundwork for sustainable peace.

Addressing Societal Healing Through Acknowledgment and Dialogue

At the heart of restorative justice is the process of acknowledgment. Acknowledging the harm caused by atrocities is a critical step in validating the experiences of victims and restoring their dignity. Perpetrators are encouraged to take responsibility for their actions, offering apologies or symbolic reparations that recognize the suffering they have caused.

Dialogue is another cornerstone of restorative justice. Facilitated discussions between victims, perpetrators, and community members provide an opportunity for open communication, fostering understanding and empathy. These dialogues can help dispel mistrust, reduce the dehumanization of opposing groups, and pave the way for reconciliation. In deeply divided societies, these processes can act as a powerful antidote to cycles of violence and retribution.

The Complementary Role of Restorative Justice in Transitional Justice Systems

In transitional justice systems, restorative justice complements retributive mechanisms by addressing the broader needs of post-conflict societies. Truth commissions, for example, integrate restorative principles by providing platforms for survivors to share their stories and for communities to confront their collective histories. Reparations programs, which acknowledge and address the harm caused to victims, also embody restorative ideals by fostering healing and empowerment.

The integration of restorative justice into transitional frameworks ensures a more holistic approach to post-conflict recovery. By addressing both individual and societal dimensions of harm, restorative justice helps to rebuild trust, foster reconciliation, and lay the foundation for enduring peace.

In short, restorative justice expands the boundaries of traditional justice systems, emphasizing acknowledgment, dialogue, and relationship-building as essential components of post-conflict recovery. By complementing retributive mechanisms, it addresses the human and societal dimensions of justice, ensuring that the pursuit of accountability is accompanied by efforts to heal and restore. As the chapter progresses, the focus will turn to specific restorative mechanisms, such as truth commissions and reparations, which exemplify these principles in action.

8.2 Truth Commissions: Lessons in Acknowledgment

Truth commissions are vital restorative mechanisms in post-conflict societies, offering a platform for survivors, perpetrators, and communities to confront their shared histories. Unlike courts that focus on legal culpability, truth commissions emphasize acknowledgment and understanding of the broader patterns of violence, aiming to foster healing and reconciliation. These commissions play a pivotal role in uncovering the truth about past atrocities, validating victims' experiences, and promoting societal reflection. By addressing collective harm and laying bare the truths of systemic injustices, they help rebuild trust and pave the way for sustainable peace.

The Role of Truth Commissions in Post-Conflict Societies

Truth commissions provide a structured process for documenting and acknowledging the human cost of conflict. Their objectives often include investigating human rights violations, identifying root causes of violence, and recommending measures for reparations and institutional reforms. In doing so, they bridge the gap between retributive justice and reconciliation by prioritizing acknowledgment over punishment.

The strength of truth commissions lies in their ability to give voice to victims and survivors, offering them an opportunity to share their stories publicly. For many, this process is a form of justice in itself, restoring their dignity and ensuring that their suffering is not forgotten. Perpetrators are also encouraged to participate, offering confessions or apologies that can contribute to the healing process. Through these efforts, truth commissions foster accountability without resorting to punitive measures, emphasizing the importance of societal transformation.

Case Studies: South Africa and Sierra Leone

Two prominent examples of truth commissions—South Africa's Truth and Reconciliation Commission (TRC) and Sierra Leone's Truth and Reconciliation Commission—demonstrate the power of truth-telling in addressing post-conflict challenges.

South Africa's Truth and Reconciliation Commission: Established in the aftermath of apartheid, South Africa's TRC became a global symbol of restorative justice. Victims and perpetrators participated in public hearings, sharing their experiences and acknowledging wrongdoing. The TRC balanced its focus on truth-telling with amnesty provisions, offering immunity to those who fully disclosed their crimes. While not without criticism, the TRC fostered national reflection, brought hidden atrocities to light, and laid the groundwork for reconciliation in a deeply divided society.

Sierra Leone's Truth and Reconciliation Commission: Following a brutal civil war marked by mass killings, sexual violence, and child soldier recruitment, Sierra Leone's TRC sought to address the nation's trauma and promote reconciliation. It documented extensive human rights violations, provided victims with a platform to share their stories, and included the perspectives of children and marginalized groups. The TRC emphasized the importance of reparations and institutional reforms to prevent future violence, demonstrating the potential of truth commissions to contribute to long-term stability.

The Power of Truth-Telling in Rebuilding Trust

Truth-telling is a cornerstone of truth commissions, providing a path toward rebuilding trust in fractured societies. By publicly acknowledging atrocities, these mechanisms validate victims' experiences and affirm their place in the post-conflict narrative. This acknowledgment fosters collective healing and helps repair relationships between divided communities.

Truth-telling also plays a preventive role by exposing the root causes and systemic patterns of violence. In doing so, it raises awareness of the societal conditions that enable conflict, encouraging reforms that address inequalities and injustices. By confronting the past openly and honestly, truth commissions help societies move beyond denial and avoidance, creating a foundation for lasting peace.

In summary, truth commissions are indispensable tools for post-conflict recovery, emphasizing acknowledgment and healing over retribution. Through their focus on truth-telling, these mechanisms provide a space for survivors and perpetrators to confront their shared histories, fostering accountability and reconciliation. As the chapter progresses, the discussion will turn to reparations as another critical restorative mechanism, highlighting how these measures restore dignity to victims and contribute to societal healing.

8.3 Reparation Mechanisms: Restoring Dignity to Victims

Reparations are a cornerstone of restorative justice, designed to acknowledge harm, restore dignity, and provide redress to victims of atrocities. Whether financial, symbolic, or community-based, reparations play a critical role in addressing the legacies of violence and rebuilding trust in post-conflict societies. Beyond compensating for material losses, reparations offer victims validation and recognition, affirming their place in the rebuilding process. This section explores different forms of reparations, the challenges of balancing these initiatives with resource constraints, and examples of successful programs that have provided meaningful redress to survivors.

Financial, Symbolic, and Community-Based Reparations: What Works?

Reparations can take many forms, each addressing distinct aspects of harm caused by conflict. Financial reparations provide direct compensation to victims for losses suffered, such as land, property, or livelihoods. While straightforward in concept, financial reparations are often resource-intensive and may fail to address deeper psychological and social wounds.

Symbolic reparations, such as public apologies, commemorations, or memorials, offer acknowledgment of victims' suffering and ensure that their experiences are not forgotten. These measures, while intangible, can have profound emotional and cultural impacts, fostering healing and reconciliation.

Community-based reparations focus on rebuilding social and economic infrastructures in affected regions, benefiting entire communities rather than individual victims. Initiatives like rebuilding schools, providing healthcare, or restoring cultural sites help repair the fabric of society and address systemic inequalities exacerbated by conflict.

Effective reparation programs often combine these approaches, tailoring measures to the needs of victims and the broader community. The success of reparations lies in their ability to balance material compensation with acknowledgment and healing, ensuring that victims feel genuinely supported and valued.

Balancing Reparations with Resource Limitations in Post-Conflict Societies

Implementing reparations in post-conflict societies is often fraught with resource challenges. Governments emerging from conflict may face limited budgets, damaged infrastructure, and competing priorities, making it difficult to allocate sufficient funds for reparations. Balancing the need for reparations with broader reconstruction efforts requires innovative strategies and international support.

One approach is to prioritize symbolic and community-based reparations, which often cost less than direct financial compensation but have far-reaching impacts. Public acknowledgments, educational reforms, and communal infrastructure projects can provide significant redress while fostering social cohesion and long-term development.

International funding and partnerships can also play a critical role in supporting reparation initiatives. Donor nations, global institutions, and NGOs can provide financial assistance, technical expertise, and advocacy to ensure that reparation programs are implemented effectively and equitably.

Examples of Successful Reparation Initiatives

Several historical examples highlight how reparations have restored dignity to victims and contributed to societal healing:

Germany's Compensation for Holocaust Survivors: In the aftermath of World War II, Germany implemented comprehensive reparation programs for Holocaust survivors, including financial compensation, pensions, and healthcare benefits. These measures provided material support while acknowledging the immense suffering caused by the Nazi regime. The program set a precedent for state responsibility in addressing historical injustices and remains a model for reparation initiatives worldwide.

Colombia's Reparations for Civil War Victims: Following decades of armed conflict, Colombia's government established the Victims' Law in 2011, which included provisions for reparations to survivors of violence. The program combined financial compensation with symbolic measures, such as public apologies and commemorations, and community-based initiatives to rebuild affected regions. By integrating restorative and transformative elements, Colombia's approach demonstrated the potential of reparations to address both individual and collective harms.

Thus, reparations are a vital component of restorative justice, offering victims acknowledgment, validation, and support while contributing to societal healing and reconstruction. Whether financial, symbolic, or community-based, these measures help repair the physical, emotional, and social wounds of conflict. By examining successful initiatives such as Germany's Holocaust reparations and Colombia's post-conflict programs, this section highlights the transformative potential of reparations in restoring dignity to victims and fostering sustainable peace. As the chapter progresses, the discussion will shift to reconciliation practices, emphasizing how bridging divides can build resilient communities in the wake of conflict.

8.4 Reconciliation in Practice: Building Bridges Between Communities

Reconciliation is a cornerstone of post-conflict recovery, focusing on rebuilding trust, fostering understanding, and mending the divides that violence leaves behind. It goes beyond institutional mechanisms, relying on the active participation of individuals and communities to create a shared vision for the future. Through education, cultural exchange, and grassroots initiatives, reconciliation seeks to heal intergenerational trauma and address the lingering scars of conflict. However, the delicate balance between justice and forgiveness remains a critical question: can reconciliation truly succeed without accountability? This section explores practical approaches to reconciliation, addressing the complexities and possibilities of uniting fractured societies.

Reconciliation Through Education, Cultural Exchange, and Local Initiatives

Education and cultural exchange are powerful tools for fostering reconciliation in post-conflict societies. Schools and universities can play a critical role in promoting understanding by teaching inclusive histories that acknowledge past atrocities and emphasize shared humanity. Educational curricula that incorporate multiple perspectives on conflict encourage critical thinking and help dismantle the narratives of division and hatred that fuel violence.

Cultural exchange initiatives, such as art exhibits, music festivals, and storytelling programs, provide platforms for dialogue and mutual understanding. By celebrating shared traditions and creating opportunities for interaction, these efforts build bridges between divided communities and reinforce the values of tolerance and coexistence.

Local initiatives, often led by grassroots organizations, are equally vital. Community-led dialogues, peacebuilding workshops, and intergroup collaborations address grievances at a personal level, creating spaces for honest communication and collective problem-solving. These efforts are particularly effective in regions where formal reconciliation mechanisms may feel distant or inaccessible.

Addressing Intergenerational Trauma in Post-Conflict Societies

The impact of conflict extends far beyond its immediate victims, affecting subsequent generations through intergenerational trauma. Children and grandchildren of those who experienced violence often inherit the psychological and emotional burdens of unresolved conflict, perpetuating cycles of mistrust and division.

Addressing intergenerational trauma requires holistic approaches that combine psychological support with community-based interventions. Mental health services tailored to the needs of affected populations can help individuals process their experiences and build resilience. At the community level, initiatives that encourage collective storytelling and commemoration provide opportunities for shared healing, ensuring that the legacy of conflict does not define future generations.

Balancing Justice and Forgiveness: Can Reconciliation Succeed Without Accountability?

The relationship between justice and forgiveness is one of the most complex aspects of reconciliation. While forgiveness can pave the way for healing, it often requires acknowledgment and accountability as its foundation. Victims and survivors may struggle to reconcile with those responsible for atrocities if there is no admission of guilt or meaningful effort to make amends.

In some contexts, reconciliation efforts have succeeded by integrating restorative justice principles, where perpetrators are encouraged to confess their crimes and engage directly with victims. This approach fosters understanding and empathy, allowing communities to move forward together. However, when accountability is absent, reconciliation risks being perceived as superficial or forced, potentially deepening divisions rather than healing them.

Balancing justice and forgiveness requires context-sensitive strategies that reflect the needs and expectations of affected communities. While accountability is essential for many, others may prioritize forgiveness and moving forward over punitive measures. Successful reconciliation efforts recognize and accommodate these diverse perspectives, ensuring that both justice and forgiveness are tools for healing rather than sources of further conflict.

In summary, reconciliation is a deeply personal and collective process that seeks to bridge divides and foster unity in the aftermath of conflict. Through education, cultural exchange, and local initiatives, communities can create spaces for healing and understanding. Addressing intergenerational trauma and balancing the complex relationship between justice and forgiveness are critical components of this journey. As the chapter progresses, the discussion will focus on the role of global institutions and mechanisms in supporting reconciliation efforts, highlighting how they can complement local practices to build sustainable peace.

8.5 The Role of Global Institutions in Restorative Justice

Global institutions play a pivotal role in advancing restorative justice by providing the frameworks, resources, and legitimacy necessary for post-conflict recovery. While local initiatives address immediate community needs, international mechanisms like the **International Criminal Court (ICC)**, hybrid courts, and global organizations ensure that reconciliation efforts are supported and integrated into broader accountability frameworks. This section examines how these institutions facilitate reconciliation alongside prosecution, support truth commissions and reparations, and align global justice mechanisms with local reconciliation efforts to create a cohesive approach to healing and justice.

The ICC and Hybrid Courts: Facilitating Reconciliation Alongside Prosecution

The ICC and hybrid courts are central to the global justice system, balancing retributive and restorative justice principles. While the ICC focuses on prosecuting individuals responsible for war crimes, crimes against humanity, and genocide, its work indirectly supports reconciliation by addressing impunity and ensuring accountability for the most egregious violations. By holding perpetrators accountable, the ICC validates victims' experiences and establishes a foundation for rebuilding trust within affected communities.

Hybrid courts, such as the **Extraordinary Chambers in the Courts of Cambodia** or the **Special Court for Sierra Leone**, combine international expertise with local participation, bridging the gap between global standards and local contexts. These courts often incorporate restorative elements, such as encouraging dialogue between victims and perpetrators or recommending reparations as part of sentencing. By integrating local voices into judicial processes, hybrid courts foster a sense of ownership and relevance, enhancing their impact on reconciliation efforts.

The Role of International Organizations in Supporting Truth Commissions and Reparations

International organizations such as the **United Nations**, **World Bank**, and **NGOs** play a critical role in supporting truth commissions and reparations, ensuring these mechanisms have the resources and legitimacy needed to succeed. Truth commissions often require significant logistical, financial, and technical support to conduct investigations, collect testimonies, and produce comprehensive reports. Organizations like the **UN Development Programme (UNDP)** provide training for investigators, funding for operations, and expertise in designing truth-telling processes that are culturally sensitive and inclusive.

In the realm of reparations, international organizations often facilitate funding and implementation, particularly in resource-constrained post-conflict societies. For example, the **International Organization for Migration (IOM)** has supported reparations programs for displaced populations, helping to address the material and symbolic needs of victims. These organizations also play an advocacy role, ensuring that reparations remain a priority in peace agreements and reconstruction efforts.

Aligning Global Justice Mechanisms with Local Reconciliation Efforts

For restorative justice to succeed, global mechanisms must align with local reconciliation initiatives. This alignment ensures that international efforts do not overshadow or conflict with community-based approaches, which are often more accessible and culturally relevant to victims.

One way to achieve this alignment is through partnerships between international institutions and local organizations. For instance, the ICC's outreach programs aim to engage communities directly affected by its cases, providing updates on proceedings and creating platforms for dialogue. Similarly, hybrid courts often include local judges or advisors, ensuring that global standards are adapted to reflect local realities.

Another key strategy is the integration of local practices into global frameworks. For example, the use of **Gacaca courts** in Rwanda complemented the work of the ICTR by addressing lower-level crimes through community-based processes. This dual approach allowed for both formal accountability and grassroots reconciliation, creating a more comprehensive justice ecosystem.

In conclusion, global institutions are essential to restorative justice, providing the expertise, resources, and legitimacy needed to complement local reconciliation efforts. The ICC and hybrid courts balance prosecution with reconciliation, while international organizations support truth commissions and reparations through funding, advocacy, and technical assistance. Aligning global mechanisms with local initiatives ensures that restorative justice is both inclusive and effective, addressing the diverse needs of victims and communities. As the chapter concludes, the discussion will turn to how restorative justice contributes to long-term peace and stability, emphasizing its role in creating a foundation for sustainable reconciliation.

8.6 Toward Sustainable Peace: Restorative Justice as a Framework

Restorative justice is more than a post-conflict mechanism; it is a transformative framework that lays the foundation for sustainable peace and stability. By addressing the root causes of conflict, fostering reconciliation, and rebuilding relationships, restorative justice moves societies beyond the immediate aftermath of violence toward a future defined by unity and resilience. This section explores how restorative justice contributes to long-term peace, highlights lessons learned from integrating restorative and retributive approaches, and sets the stage for reforming global justice systems to address the complexities of modern conflicts.

How Restorative Justice Contributes to Long-Term Peace and Stability

Restorative justice fosters peace by addressing the deeper wounds of conflict that traditional retributive mechanisms often overlook. It prioritizes acknowledgment, healing, and the restoration of relationships, ensuring that victims, perpetrators, and communities alike are part of the recovery process. This inclusivity helps dismantle cycles of mistrust and resentment, replacing them with dialogue and mutual understanding.

By emphasizing collective healing, restorative justice also strengthens the social fabric of post-conflict societies. Community-based initiatives, such as truth-telling processes and reparations, promote a shared sense of accountability and responsibility, reducing the likelihood of renewed violence. Furthermore, restorative justice's focus on education and cultural exchange helps reshape societal norms, fostering tolerance and coexistence among future generations.

Lessons Learned for Integrating Restorative and Retributive Justice

While restorative justice offers transformative potential, its success often depends on how well it is integrated with retributive mechanisms. Key lessons from past initiatives highlight the importance of balance and complementarity between these approaches:

Acknowledgment and Accountability: Effective justice systems must ensure that perpetrators are held accountable while also providing space for acknowledgment and reconciliation. The combination of formal prosecutions with truth commissions, as seen in South Africa, demonstrates how these mechanisms can work in tandem to deliver holistic justice.

Victim-Centric Approaches: Placing victims at the center of justice processes ensures their needs and voices are prioritized. Reparations, public apologies, and opportunities for victims to share their stories foster empowerment and dignity, addressing the emotional and psychological dimensions of recovery.

Flexibility and Context Sensitivity: No single model of justice fits all contexts. Successful integration of restorative and retributive mechanisms requires flexibility to adapt to the unique cultural, political, and social dynamics of each society. Hybrid courts, for example, have proven effective in bridging global standards with local realities.

Commitment to Long-Term Engagement: Restorative justice is not a one-time process but a long-term commitment to building trust and stability. Continued investment in education, community dialogue, and institutional reforms ensures that the gains of restorative justice are sustained over time.

Conclusion

Healing the wounds of conflict requires a holistic approach that addresses both the tangible and intangible dimensions of recovery. Reparations and rebuilding efforts provide victims with material support and validation, while truth-telling and acknowledgment of atrocities foster emotional healing and societal trust. These mechanisms, rooted in restorative justice, demonstrate that reconciliation is not a passive process but an active commitment to addressing the legacies of violence and division.

This chapter has explored how justice, when implemented with compassion and inclusivity, can pave the way for peace. By balancing accountability with healing and focusing on rebuilding relationships and communities, justice becomes a bridge to sustainable reconciliation. As the book transitions to its final chapter, attention will turn to the future of international justice, examining how evolving mechanisms and technologies can uphold these principles in an increasingly complex and interconnected world.

9. Healing Wounds: Toward Reconciliation

As the pursuit of justice seeks to hold perpetrators accountable and uphold the principles of accountability, the broader goal of healing societies fractured by conflict becomes equally urgent. Justice is not merely about retribution; it is about paving the way for reconciliation, fostering understanding, and rebuilding trust. This chapter transitions from the mechanisms of justice explored earlier to the human-centered processes of reconciliation, focusing on reparations, truth-telling, and the role of justice in fostering peace. By addressing the physical, emotional, and societal scars left by conflict, reconciliation offers a path toward sustainable peace and stability, ensuring that societies can move forward together without forgetting the lessons of the past.

9.1 Reparations and Rebuilding After Conflict

Rebuilding a society after conflict is a multidimensional process that extends beyond immediate humanitarian relief. It requires addressing physical destruction, restoring livelihoods, and healing the psychological and social scars left by violence. Reparations and reconstruction serve as vital components of this recovery, providing tangible acknowledgments of harm suffered while laying the groundwork for sustainable peace. This section delves into the forms of reparations—financial, symbolic, and structural—alongside the challenges and strategies involved in reconstructing infrastructure and restoring livelihoods amid limited resources.

Financial, Symbolic, and Structural Reparations: Addressing Victims' Needs

Reparations are essential tools for recognizing and addressing the suffering endured by victims of conflict. They provide a means of acknowledging past wrongs while supporting the recovery and resilience of affected individuals and communities. Reparations typically take three primary forms:

Financial Reparations: Financial compensation provides direct monetary support to individuals or communities affected by conflict. These reparations address economic losses, personal injuries, and damages to property, helping victims rebuild their lives. Funds may cover medical treatment, education, housing, or livelihood restoration, offering immediate relief and long-term opportunities.

Symbolic Reparations: Symbolic gestures acknowledge the moral and emotional dimensions of harm, validating victims' experiences. Public apologies, memorials, and commemorative events serve as reminders of past injustices while fostering a culture of remembrance and reconciliation. These non-material actions contribute significantly to emotional healing and collective acknowledgment.

Structural Reparations: Structural reparations focus on institutional reforms to address systemic issues that may have contributed to conflict. These efforts include revising laws, reforming governance structures, and implementing measures to uphold human rights and the rule of law. Structural reparations aim to prevent future conflicts by creating more equitable and inclusive societies.

A comprehensive approach to reparations combines these elements, addressing immediate needs through financial support, validating victims through symbolic gestures, and fostering long-term stability through systemic reforms. Together, these measures contribute to rebuilding trust between citizens and the state, laying a foundation for lasting peace and reconciliation.

Reconstructing Infrastructure and Restoring Livelihoods

The physical devastation caused by conflict often leaves communities struggling to rebuild essential infrastructure and regain economic stability. Reconstruction efforts focus on restoring vital facilities such as roads, bridges, schools, hospitals, and utilities, which are critical for the resumption of normal life. Effective reconstruction involves:

✓ **Damage Assessment and Prioritization:** Conducting comprehensive assessments to identify critical needs ensures that resources are allocated strategically and address the most urgent requirements.

✓ **Community Participation:** Engaging local communities in planning and implementation fosters a sense of ownership and ensures that reconstruction projects align with their priorities.

✓ **Sustainable Practices:** Rebuilding infrastructure with resilience in mind—incorporating disaster-resistant materials and environmentally sustainable methods—prepares communities for future challenges.

Restoring livelihoods is equally critical to long-term recovery. Economic stability reduces dependency on aid and fosters self-reliance, which is essential for rebuilding trust and resilience. Key strategies include:

✓ **Supporting Small Enterprises and Agriculture:** Providing microloans, grants, and technical training to farmers and entrepreneurs stimulates local economies and generates employment opportunities.

✓ **Vocational Training and Education:** Equipping individuals with practical skills enhances their ability to secure employment and participate actively in rebuilding their communities.

✓ **Rebuilding Supply Chains and Market Access:** Restoring trade networks and providing infrastructure for commerce enable producers to reenter markets, revitalizing economic activity.

Reconstruction and livelihood restoration not only address material needs but also contribute to psychological recovery by restoring a sense of normalcy and hope.

Challenges in Balancing Limited Resources with Comprehensive Recovery

Post-conflict societies often face significant resource constraints, making it difficult to meet the extensive needs of recovery. Common challenges include:

✓ **Resource Allocation:** Striking a balance between immediate humanitarian needs and long-term development goals requires careful prioritization and efficient use of funds.

✓ **Donor Dependency and Coordination:** Reliance on international donors introduces challenges related to aligning donor priorities with local needs and ensuring sustainable funding.

✓ **Institutional Weaknesses:** Limited institutional capacity can hinder the planning and execution of recovery efforts. Strengthening governance structures and administrative competencies is essential.

✓ **Ensuring Equity and Inclusion:** Marginalized groups, including women, ethnic minorities, and displaced persons, often face barriers to accessing assistance. Inclusive approaches ensure that recovery efforts benefit all affected populations.

✓ **Addressing Corruption and Mismanagement:** Transparency and accountability mechanisms are necessary to prevent corruption and ensure that resources reach intended beneficiaries.

Strategies for Effective Recovery

To overcome these challenges, post-conflict societies must adopt strategic and coordinated approaches:

✓ **Integrated Planning:** Aligning humanitarian aid with development goals ensures a cohesive approach to recovery. Collaboration among governments, international organizations, and civil society enhances effectiveness.

✓ **Leveraging Technology:** Digital tools for needs assessment, project monitoring, and transparent reporting improve efficiency and accountability.

✓ **Strengthening Institutions:** Building institutional capacity enables better resource management and enhances the delivery of essential services.

✓ **Public-Private Partnerships:** Engaging the private sector mobilizes additional resources and expertise, accelerating infrastructure projects and economic revitalization.

✓ **Promoting Inclusivity:** Ensuring that programs address the needs of vulnerable groups fosters equity and prevents further marginalization.

Thus, reparations and reconstruction are critical for rebuilding trust, restoring stability, and promoting reconciliation in post-conflict societies. Financial, symbolic, and structural reparations provide victims with acknowledgment and support, while the reconstruction of infrastructure and livelihoods fosters economic resilience and psychological recovery. However, limited resources and competing priorities present significant challenges, requiring innovative strategies and collaboration among stakeholders.

By integrating these efforts into a holistic recovery framework, societies can address the legacies of conflict while building a foundation for sustainable peace. As the chapter progresses, attention will shift to the role of truth-telling and acknowledgment in fostering healing and preventing the recurrence of violence. Together, reparations, rebuilding, and truth-telling form a comprehensive approach to reconciliation, demonstrating that justice is as much about healing as it is about accountability.

9.2 The Power of Truth-Telling and Acknowledgment

Truth-telling and acknowledgment are essential for healing the wounds of conflict and rebuilding fractured societies. They validate victims' experiences, foster understanding, and confront the legacies of violence that often linger long after hostilities end. By addressing the past openly and honestly, societies can forge pathways for reconciliation and lay the groundwork for sustainable peace. This section delves into the role of acknowledging atrocities in the healing process, examines truth commissions as platforms for survivors and communities, and explores the critical importance of public acknowledgment in preventing future violence.

Acknowledging Atrocities as a Foundation for Healing

Acknowledgment is a vital first step toward reconciliation and recovery. When societies openly recognize the atrocities of the past, they validate the pain and suffering of victims, restoring dignity and affirming their place in the post-conflict narrative. Acknowledgment helps counter denial and revisionism, ensuring that the truth is preserved for future generations and preventing the erasure of historical injustices.

For victims, acknowledgment serves as a form of justice that extends beyond legal rulings. Hearing their stories recognized by society and leadership provides a sense of validation and helps them begin the process of healing. For perpetrators and broader communities, acknowledgment fosters accountability and reflection, encouraging steps toward rehabilitation and reconciliation.

Truth Commissions as Platforms for Survivors and Communities

Truth commissions provide structured platforms for survivors, perpetrators, and communities to confront their shared histories. These commissions, often established outside traditional judicial frameworks, focus on uncovering systemic patterns of violence and human rights violations rather than assigning blame or dispensing punitive measures.

By offering survivors the opportunity to share their experiences through public hearings, investigations, and detailed reports, truth commissions empower victims and give them a voice in shaping the narrative of the past. They also educate society about the causes and consequences of violence, fostering a sense of collective accountability.

For instance, **South Africa's Truth and Reconciliation Commission** became a global model for reconciliation by allowing victims and perpetrators of apartheid-era violence to present their testimonies in public forums. This process shed light on hidden atrocities and laid the foundation for national healing. Similarly, **Sierra Leone's Truth and Reconciliation Commission** amplified the voices of marginalized groups, including women and children disproportionately affected by the civil war. These commissions demonstrate the transformative power of truth-telling in addressing collective trauma and rebuilding social cohesion.

The Role of Public Acknowledgment in Preventing Future Violence

Public acknowledgment of atrocities extends beyond individual healing; it plays a crucial role in shaping societal norms and preventing future violence. When states, leaders, and communities openly recognize past wrongs, they affirm a commitment to accountability and signal that such actions will not be tolerated. This acknowledgment reinforces human rights norms, creating a deterrent against future violations.

Public acknowledgment can take various forms, including official apologies, commemorative events, and the integration of conflict histories into educational curricula. These acts serve as enduring reminders of the consequences of division and violence, fostering a culture of vigilance and prevention.

Examples of successful public acknowledgment include **Germany's ongoing reckoning with the Holocaust**, which incorporates education, memorials, and public discourse to embed a strong commitment to human rights. Similarly, **Rwanda's annual genocide memorials** ensure that the memory of the 1994 genocide remains a central part of the nation's identity, promoting unity and reconciliation.

In conclusion, truth-telling and acknowledgment are powerful tools for addressing the legacies of conflict and fostering reconciliation. They validate victims' experiences, provide platforms for collective healing, and embed lessons from the past into the societal consciousness. By confronting history openly, societies can prevent future violence and rebuild trust within divided communities. As the chapter progresses, the focus will shift to examining how justice mechanisms can complement truth-telling efforts, exploring whether accountability can pave the way for sustainable peace and reconciliation.

9.3 Justice as a Path to Peace

Justice is more than a mechanism for retribution; it is a bridge to peace, offering societies a means to address past wrongs while fostering trust and stability for the future. Balancing accountability with forgiveness is a delicate yet essential process that enables communities to move beyond cycles of violence and division. By integrating retributive and restorative approaches, justice mechanisms can support reconciliation and prevent the recurrence of conflict. This section examines how these elements intertwine to create a pathway to peace, drawing on lessons from post-conflict societies and exploring the broader role of justice in promoting long-term stability.

Balancing Accountability with Forgiveness: Lessons from Post-Conflict Societies

The tension between accountability and forgiveness represents one of the most profound challenges in post-conflict justice. While victims and societies demand accountability to acknowledge harm and restore trust, forgiveness is often necessary for rebuilding relationships and fostering reconciliation. Striking this balance requires a nuanced and culturally sensitive approach.

In **South Africa**, the Truth and Reconciliation Commission (TRC) exemplified this balance. By allowing perpetrators to seek amnesty through full disclosure of their crimes, the TRC provided a platform for acknowledgment and forgiveness. Although controversial, this approach prioritized healing and nation-building over punitive justice, facilitating the country's transition from apartheid to democracy. Similarly, in **Rwanda**, the Gacaca courts complemented the work of the International Criminal Tribunal for Rwanda (ICTR) by addressing lower-level crimes in a community-based setting. These courts encouraged dialogue and reconciliation within communities deeply scarred by the 1994 genocide.

These examples illustrate that forgiveness cannot be mandated but must emerge organically from processes that validate victims' experiences and encourage perpetrators to take responsibility for their actions. Tailoring justice mechanisms to reflect the specific needs and values of affected societies is essential for their success.

Integrating Retributive and Restorative Justice to Foster Trust

Effective justice systems integrate the strengths of both retributive and restorative approaches to address the legal, emotional, and societal dimensions of reconciliation. Retributive justice ensures formal accountability through prosecutions and trials, deterring future violations and reinforcing the rule of law. However, it often falls short in addressing the broader societal need for healing and trust-building.

Restorative justice complements retributive measures by emphasizing acknowledgment, dialogue, and the restoration of relationships. Mechanisms such as truth commissions, reparations, and community-led initiatives foster understanding and empathy, bringing victims and perpetrators together to confront the past collectively. The integration of these approaches creates a holistic justice process that strengthens trust within societies.

For example, **Sierra Leone's post-civil war recovery** utilized a hybrid model that combined the retributive focus of the Special Court for Sierra Leone with the restorative goals of its Truth and Reconciliation Commission. This dual approach addressed the individual accountability of high-ranking perpetrators while fostering collective healing in communities. By combining these elements, Sierra Leone demonstrated how justice mechanisms can work in tandem to rebuild trust and promote peace.

The Potential of Justice Mechanisms to Prevent Future Conflicts and Promote Stability

Justice mechanisms play a critical role in preventing future conflicts by addressing the root causes of violence and establishing norms of accountability. When societies witness that crimes will not go unpunished, it reinforces respect for human rights and the rule of law, deterring potential perpetrators and breaking cycles of impunity.

Justice also contributes to stability by rebuilding trust between citizens and the state. Transparent and inclusive justice processes signal a commitment to fairness and equality, addressing grievances and divisions that often fuel conflict. Reparations programs and institutional reforms, such as those implemented in **post-war Germany**, further enhance stability by addressing systemic issues and ensuring that victims feel supported and recognized.

Moreover, justice mechanisms foster opportunities for dialogue and collaboration between divided communities, promoting social cohesion. By integrating restorative elements such as truth-telling and reparations, these mechanisms ensure that the pursuit of justice not only addresses past wrongs but also fosters healing, reducing the likelihood of future violence.

In short, Justice, when approached holistically, is a powerful tool for promoting peace and stability. By balancing accountability with forgiveness, integrating retributive and restorative approaches, and addressing the root causes of conflict, justice mechanisms help societies move beyond violence and division. They establish pathways for reconciliation, rebuild trust, and create the foundation for long-term stability. As this chapter progresses, attention will turn to practical reconciliation efforts, exploring how grassroots initiatives and education can further strengthen bridges between divided communities. Together, justice and reconciliation form the bedrock of sustainable peace.

9.4 Reconciliation in Action: Bridging Divides

Reconciliation is an active and inclusive process that engages individuals, communities, and institutions in rebuilding trust and fostering understanding after conflict. It moves beyond formal justice mechanisms to address the social and cultural divides that persist long after violence ends. Grassroots initiatives, education, and cultural exchange are critical in creating spaces for dialogue, dismantling stereotypes, and promoting unity. This section highlights practical approaches to reconciliation, emphasizing the transformative potential of community-led efforts and providing global examples of successful initiatives.

Grassroots Initiatives Fostering Intergroup Dialogue and Unity

Grassroots initiatives are often the driving force behind reconciliation efforts, working directly with communities to address grievances, rebuild trust, and foster unity. These initiatives are based on the belief that reconciliation must begin at the local level, engaging those most directly affected by conflict.

In **Rwanda**, community-based dialogue programs have brought together survivors and perpetrators of the 1994 genocide to share their experiences and rebuild relationships. Facilitated by local organizations, these programs provide safe spaces for participants to confront painful truths, express remorse, and work toward mutual understanding. By promoting open communication, these initiatives help repair the social fabric of communities.

In **Northern Ireland**, cross-community youth programs have played a pivotal role in fostering reconciliation between Catholic and Protestant communities. Through shared activities such as sports, arts, and workshops, these programs break down stereotypes and build trust among young people from historically divided groups.

Grassroots initiatives succeed because they are deeply embedded in the cultural and social contexts of the communities they serve. By prioritizing empathy, collaboration, and inclusivity, they enable individuals to move beyond the legacies of violence and forge new connections.

The Role of Education and Cultural Exchange in Repairing Relationships

Education and cultural exchange are powerful tools for addressing the long-term impacts of conflict and fostering reconciliation. Schools and universities play a central role in shaping societal narratives, offering opportunities to teach inclusive histories that acknowledge multiple perspectives on conflict. By fostering critical thinking and dismantling divisive ideologies, education helps societies confront their pasts while preparing for a shared future.

In **post-apartheid South Africa**, educational reforms aimed to address racial and economic inequalities rooted in apartheid policies. Schools now include lessons on human rights and social justice, emphasizing unity and diversity as central tenets of the nation's identity.

Cultural exchange initiatives complement these efforts by providing platforms for dialogue and mutual understanding. **Arts-based reconciliation programs**, such as theater productions, music festivals, and collaborative art projects, allow individuals to express their experiences and explore shared identities. For example, the **Sarajevo Film Festival** in Bosnia and Herzegovina has become a symbol of unity, showcasing films that address themes of reconciliation, resilience, and shared humanity.

By fostering empathy and challenging stereotypes, education and cultural exchange build the foundations for lasting peace, offering societies tools to repair relationships and prevent future divisions.

Examples of Successful Reconciliation Efforts from Global Contexts

Global examples demonstrate the potential of reconciliation initiatives to transform divided societies and foster sustainable peace:

Gacaca Courts in Rwanda: Initially designed as a justice mechanism, the Gacaca courts also facilitated reconciliation by bringing communities together to address the aftermath of genocide. Their emphasis on truth-telling and reparations rebuilt trust and created a sense of collective accountability.

Truth and Reconciliation Commission (TRC) in South Africa: The TRC combined public hearings, symbolic gestures, and community engagement to confront the legacies of apartheid. By prioritizing acknowledgment and forgiveness, it helped South Africans work toward a shared and inclusive future.

Grassroots Reconciliation Efforts in Colombia: Following decades of armed conflict, Colombian organizations have fostered dialogue between former combatants, victims, and communities. Initiatives like **Memory Houses**, which preserve victims' stories, have created spaces for understanding and healing, enabling communities to address collective trauma.

These examples highlight that reconciliation is not a one-size-fits-all process. Effective initiatives are tailored to local contexts, blending traditional practices with innovative approaches to meet the unique challenges of divided societies.

In summary, reconciliation in action relies on the active participation of communities, supported by education, cultural exchange, and grassroots efforts. By fostering dialogue, promoting understanding, and bridging divides, these initiatives address the emotional and social legacies of conflict while rebuilding relationships. Global examples underscore the transformative potential of reconciliation when grounded in inclusivity and mutual respect. As the chapter progresses, the discussion will focus on integrating these efforts into a holistic framework for reconciliation, exploring how justice, reparations, and truth-telling work together to build sustainable peace.

9.5 Toward a Holistic Framework for Reconciliation

Reconciliation after conflict is a multifaceted and dynamic process that requires the integration of justice, reparations, and truth-telling. Each component addresses distinct yet interconnected needs of post-conflict societies, creating a foundation for sustainable peace. Achieving this holistic framework demands collaboration among international institutions, local actors, and affected communities, with each stakeholder playing a vital role in fostering recovery and resilience. This section examines how these elements come together, highlights the contributions of various stakeholders, and outlines lessons learned for designing effective recovery strategies.

Linking Justice, Reparations, and Truth-Telling for Sustainable Peace

A truly comprehensive approach to reconciliation weaves together the accountability provided by justice mechanisms, the acknowledgment facilitated by truth-telling, and the reparations that restore dignity to victims. Together, these elements address the complex legacies of conflict while laying the groundwork for societal healing and long-term stability.

Justice: Formal accountability mechanisms, such as trials or hybrid courts, reinforce the rule of law and deter future violations. Justice mechanisms send a clear signal that impunity will not be tolerated, rebuilding trust between citizens and institutions by ensuring that perpetrators are held accountable.

Reparations: Financial compensation, symbolic gestures, and structural reforms provide victims with tangible recognition and support. Reparations bridge the gap between acknowledgment and practical recovery by addressing material and emotional wounds, contributing to individual and community-level healing.

Truth-Telling: Truth commissions and public acknowledgment initiatives confront the past openly, validating victims' experiences and fostering collective understanding of historical injustices. By challenging narratives of denial and promoting acknowledgment, truth-telling creates the conditions for societal reconciliation and prevents the recurrence of violence.

When integrated effectively, these components form a unified framework that addresses immediate post-conflict needs while fostering long-term resilience. Linking justice, reparations, and truth-telling ensures that reconciliation efforts are inclusive, cohesive, and responsive to the complexities of post-conflict recovery.

The Role of International and Local Actors in Supporting Reconciliation

The success of reconciliation efforts hinges on the collaboration between international institutions, local actors, and civil society, each of which contributes unique strengths and perspectives to the process.

International Institutions: Global bodies such as the United Nations, the International Criminal Court (ICC), and international NGOs provide critical resources, technical expertise, and legitimacy to reconciliation efforts. These institutions support truth commissions, fund reparations programs, and facilitate justice mechanisms, ensuring that post-conflict recovery aligns with international standards.

Local Actors: Community leaders, grassroots organizations, and local governments play a pivotal role in tailoring reconciliation initiatives to the specific cultural, social, and political contexts of affected regions. Their involvement ensures that recovery efforts resonate with local populations and address their unique needs.

Partnerships: Collaborative efforts between international and local stakeholders amplify the impact of reconciliation strategies. Hybrid courts, for example, combine global expertise with local participation, bridging the gap between international standards and community engagement. Similarly, partnerships between international donors and local NGOs enhance the effectiveness of reparations and truth-telling initiatives.

By leveraging the strengths of both global and local actors, reconciliation efforts become more inclusive, adaptable, and sustainable.

Lessons Learned for Designing Effective Post-Conflict Recovery Strategies

Decades of post-conflict reconciliation efforts provide valuable insights into designing recovery strategies that are both effective and sustainable:

Context-Specific Approaches: Successful reconciliation efforts are rooted in the cultural, social, and political realities of each society. Tailoring initiatives to local contexts ensures their relevance and effectiveness.

Victim-Centered Focus: Placing victims at the center of reconciliation efforts ensures that their needs and voices guide the process. This includes prioritizing reparations, creating platforms for truth-telling, and involving victims in decision-making.

Sustained Engagement: Reconciliation is a long-term process requiring ongoing commitment. Regular follow-ups, continued funding, and adaptive strategies are essential to maintain progress and address emerging challenges.

Inclusive Participation: Engaging diverse stakeholders—women, youth, marginalized groups—fosters broader ownership of reconciliation initiatives. Inclusivity strengthens social cohesion and ensures that all voices are represented in recovery efforts.

Transparent Processes: Transparency builds trust and legitimacy. Clear communication, accessible reporting, and accountability mechanisms are crucial for ensuring that reconciliation efforts are credible and effective.

Conclusion

Reconciliation is more than a response to conflict; it is a pathway to rebuilding societies, restoring trust, and fostering sustainable peace. This chapter has explored how reparations, truth-telling, and justice mechanisms intertwine to address the multifaceted legacies of violence. By acknowledging harm, validating victims' experiences, and fostering dialogue, reconciliation provides a framework for healing both individuals and communities.

The integration of justice, reparations, and truth-telling forms the bedrock of sustainable peace, ensuring that accountability is paired with acknowledgment and support for recovery. Grassroots efforts, education, and cultural exchange amplify these initiatives, creating spaces for understanding and unity. Global examples have demonstrated the transformative power of reconciliation when approached holistically and inclusively.

As we move to the next chapter, attention will turn to the future of international justice, focusing on how global systems can adapt to the complexities of modern conflicts. This transition underscores the necessity of innovation and collaboration to ensure that reconciliation remains central to addressing the challenges of an interconnected world.

10. The Future of International Justice

As global conflicts evolve in complexity and scale, the mechanisms of international justice must adapt to meet the challenges of modern warfare. The principles established by past tribunals and justice systems have laid a strong foundation, but contemporary realities—ranging from technological advancements to geopolitical tensions—demand innovative approaches. This chapter explores the future of international justice, focusing on reforming global systems, strengthening accountability frameworks, and leveraging emerging technologies like artificial intelligence to ensure that justice remains a cornerstone of global governance. By anticipating challenges and embracing innovation, the international community can build a resilient and equitable system capable of addressing the demands of an increasingly interconnected and complex world.

10.1 Reforming Global Justice Systems for Modern Conflicts

The global justice system, rooted in principles of accountability and fairness, faces mounting challenges in addressing the realities of modern conflicts. Contemporary warfare—marked by the rise of non-state actors, hybrid tactics, and cyber operations—demands an adaptive approach to international justice. Additionally, geopolitical complexities, jurisdictional barriers, and a lack of inclusivity in global institutions highlight the urgent need for reform. This section explores how international frameworks can evolve to meet these challenges, enhance representation, and navigate the political and jurisdictional obstacles that hinder accountability.

Adapting International Frameworks to Address Contemporary Warfare

Modern conflicts often defy traditional definitions of warfare, involving cyberattacks, targeted civilian harm, and unconventional tactics that expose the limitations of existing legal frameworks. Historically designed to address state-led and conventional military operations, these frameworks must evolve to remain relevant in today's context.

Expanding Legal Definitions: International legal frameworks must broaden their scope to include emerging warfare tactics such as cyber operations, the use of autonomous weapons, and hybrid strategies involving disinformation and economic coercion. Establishing clear guidelines ensures that perpetrators of these unconventional crimes are held accountable within a robust legal framework.

Enhancing Real-Time Response Mechanisms: Modern conflicts often require immediate intervention to prevent atrocities and preserve evidence. Strengthening international investigative and prosecutorial mechanisms to function in real-time—rather than post-conflict—ensures timely accountability and more effective justice outcomes.

Strengthening Civilian Protections: As civilians increasingly bear the brunt of modern warfare, legal frameworks must prioritize protections against forced displacement, attacks on infrastructure, and the use of banned weapons. Enhanced measures are needed to hold violators accountable for disproportionate harm to non-combatants.

Enhancing Inclusivity and Representation in Global Justice Institutions

The effectiveness and legitimacy of international justice systems depend on their inclusivity and diversity. Historically dominated by a limited set of global powers, institutions such as the International Criminal Court (ICC) and the United Nations Security Council (UNSC) have faced criticism for perceived bias and underrepresentation of key regions and marginalized groups.

Broadening Membership: Expanding the membership of global justice institutions to include historically underrepresented regions, such as Africa, Latin America, and the Global South, creates a more equitable system. Inclusive membership ensures that accountability mechanisms reflect diverse global perspectives.

Diverse Leadership and Participation: Promoting leadership roles for women, marginalized communities, and affected populations fosters trust and enhances the credibility of justice systems. Representation ensures that the voices of those most impacted by conflicts are integral to decision-making processes.

Decentralizing Power Dynamics: Reducing the dominance of a few powerful states, particularly in institutions like the UNSC where veto power often obstructs justice, can mitigate geopolitical biases. Reforms that limit or condition veto use in cases of mass atrocities ensure that justice mechanisms prioritize global interests over national agendas.

Overcoming Political and Jurisdictional Challenges in Modern Accountability

Political resistance and jurisdictional limitations remain significant obstacles to prosecuting war crimes and atrocities. States implicated in conflicts often invoke sovereignty to resist external intervention, while powerful nations leverage their influence to shield allies or themselves from accountability.

Reforming Sovereignty Norms: Establishing clear criteria for international intervention in cases of mass atrocities strikes a balance between respecting state sovereignty and ensuring accountability. These norms must emphasize that sovereignty cannot shield perpetrators of crimes against humanity.

Strengthening Universal Jurisdiction: Expanding the application of universal jurisdiction—allowing states to prosecute grave crimes regardless of where they occur—closes jurisdictional loopholes that enable impunity. Universal jurisdiction reinforces the principle that accountability transcends borders.

Enhancing Enforcement Mechanisms: Developing international task forces or regional coalitions dedicated to enforcing arrest warrants and ensuring compliance with rulings strengthens accountability. These mechanisms address the reliance on voluntary state cooperation, which often limits enforcement.

Building Political Consensus: Mobilizing global support through advocacy, multilateral partnerships, and diplomatic pressure ensures that political interests do not obstruct accountability. Transparency and consistent application of justice principles can counter accusations of selective prosecution.

In short, reforming global justice systems is critical to addressing the challenges of modern conflicts. By adapting legal frameworks to contemporary warfare, enhancing inclusivity and representation, and overcoming political and jurisdictional barriers, the international community can create a justice system that is both resilient and equitable. These reforms not only address the complexities of emerging conflicts but also reinforce global trust in accountability mechanisms. As this chapter progresses, the focus shifts to strengthening legal mechanisms, exploring how they can evolve to meet the demands of a rapidly changing world.

10.2 Strengthening Legal Mechanisms for Accountability

Ensuring accountability for war crimes and atrocities demands robust legal mechanisms capable of addressing the complexities of modern conflicts. While institutions like the International Criminal Court (ICC) and regional courts play pivotal roles, gaps in jurisdiction, enforcement, and victim inclusion often limit their effectiveness. Strengthening these mechanisms is essential to uphold the principles of justice, rebuild trust, and establish a foundation for sustainable peace. This section examines strategies to expand the jurisdiction of international courts, address enforcement challenges, and integrate victim-centric approaches into global legal frameworks.

Expanding the Jurisdiction and Reach of the ICC and Regional Courts

The ICC, established to prosecute genocide, war crimes, and crimes against humanity, operates within the constraints of its jurisdiction. Non-signatory states, including major powers like the United States, Russia, and China, remain beyond its reach, creating significant gaps in global accountability. Similarly, regional courts often face challenges related to funding, political will, and jurisdictional scope, limiting their capacity to address localized conflicts effectively.

To enhance the reach and efficacy of these courts:

Broader Ratification of the Rome Statute: Encouraging more states to ratify the Rome Statute would strengthen the ICC's global mandate. Diplomatic engagement, advocacy campaigns, and incentives for non-member states to join can increase its jurisdiction and effectiveness.

Strengthening Regional Courts: Regional courts, such as the African Court on Human and Peoples' Rights, play a vital role in addressing localized conflicts. Providing these courts with additional resources, technical assistance, and political support enhances their capacity to complement the ICC by addressing cases that fall outside its jurisdiction.

Establishing Hybrid Courts: Hybrid courts that combine international expertise with local participation bridge the gap between global standards and community needs. These courts offer a flexible and culturally sensitive approach, ensuring accountability in contexts where the ICC or regional courts face barriers.

By expanding the jurisdiction and capabilities of both international and regional courts, the global justice system can become more inclusive and adaptable to diverse conflict scenarios.

Addressing Enforcement Challenges in Prosecuting War Crimes

Enforcement remains one of the most significant obstacles to accountability in international justice. Arrest warrants, indictments, and rulings often go unexecuted due to political resistance, lack of cooperation, and limited enforcement mechanisms.

To overcome these challenges:

International Task Forces: Specialized task forces with international mandates can execute arrest warrants and enforce rulings. These units, operating under the United Nations or regional coalitions, ensure that justice mechanisms are not undermined by state inaction.

Economic and Diplomatic Tools: Sanctions, travel bans, and asset freezes against individuals and states obstructing justice create tangible consequences and pressure for compliance. Diplomatic isolation can further incentivize cooperation with international rulings.

Enhanced Cooperation Frameworks: Strengthening agreements between international courts and member states fosters greater collaboration in arresting suspects, providing evidence, and enforcing decisions. Clear protocols and mutual accountability are key to effective partnerships.

Innovative Enforcement Mechanisms: Exploring alternative approaches, such as cross-border cooperation or compliance incentives, can address enforcement gaps, particularly in cases involving powerful or uncooperative states.

Effective enforcement ensures that justice mechanisms remain credible and reinforces the principle that no individual or state is above the law.

Integrating Victim-Centric Approaches into Global Legal Frameworks

Justice mechanisms often prioritize prosecuting perpetrators but risk neglecting the needs and voices of victims. A victim-centric approach ensures that justice processes are inclusive, equitable, and restorative, addressing the harm inflicted on individuals and communities.

Key components of a victim-centric framework include:

Ensuring Victim Participation: Platforms for victims to share their stories, contribute to evidence collection, and participate in trials validate their experiences and empower them in the justice process. Truth commissions and hybrid courts often serve as effective avenues for victim engagement.

Reparations Programs: Reparations, including financial compensation, symbolic gestures, and community-based initiatives, address the material and emotional harm suffered by victims. These programs provide tangible recognition and support for recovery.

Psycho-Social Support: Integrating psychological and social support services into justice mechanisms ensures the well-being of victims, helping them navigate the trauma of conflict. These services should be prioritized as part of post-conflict recovery.

Victim-Centered Advocacy: Advocacy groups and NGOs play a critical role in representing victims' interests within international courts. Their involvement enhances the inclusivity and fairness of legal processes, ensuring that victims remain at the heart of accountability efforts.

By centering victims in justice mechanisms, the global community can foster healing, rebuild trust, and reinforce the legitimacy of legal frameworks.

In summary, strengthening legal mechanisms for accountability is vital for addressing the complexities of modern conflicts. Expanding the jurisdiction and reach of the ICC and regional courts, addressing enforcement challenges, and integrating victim-centric approaches ensure that justice mechanisms are both effective and inclusive. These reforms uphold the principles of fairness, equity, and accountability, laying the foundation for sustainable peace. As this chapter progresses, attention will shift to the transformative role of technology in advancing international justice, exploring how digital tools and artificial intelligence can revolutionize the pursuit of accountability.

10.3 The Role of AI and Digital Tools in War Crimes Prosecution

The integration of artificial intelligence (AI) and digital tools has transformed the way war crimes are documented, analyzed, and prosecuted. These technologies offer unprecedented opportunities to enhance the efficiency, accuracy, and transparency of justice processes, particularly in addressing the complexities of modern conflicts. From analyzing vast amounts of evidence to ensuring the authenticity of digital materials, AI and blockchain technologies are reshaping the landscape of international justice. However, their use also raises critical ethical and legal questions that require careful consideration. This section explores the transformative role of these technologies, emphasizing their potential while addressing the challenges they present.

Leveraging Artificial Intelligence for Evidence Analysis and Case Building

AI has become an indispensable tool for managing the immense volumes of evidence generated during conflicts. Traditional methods of evidence processing are often time-consuming and resource-intensive, but AI-driven tools streamline these processes, enabling investigators to build cases more efficiently and comprehensively.

Pattern Recognition: AI algorithms can analyze large datasets, such as satellite imagery, videos, and social media content, to identify patterns of violations, including troop movements or deliberate attacks on civilian infrastructure. This capability is invaluable for detecting systematic crimes like genocide and ethnic cleansing.

Automated Evidence Sorting: By categorizing digital evidence, such as photos, videos, and documents, based on relevance and reliability, AI reduces the workload on investigators. This allows them to focus on high-priority aspects of case building, enhancing the speed and precision of justice processes.

Natural Language Processing (NLP): NLP tools process multilingual documents and transcripts, identifying key themes, connections, and testimonies. This is particularly valuable in conflicts involving diverse linguistic and cultural contexts, ensuring that all voices are heard and represented.

Predictive Analysis: AI can analyze past patterns and real-time data to predict future violations, enabling preventive measures and rapid responses. This proactive approach aligns with the broader goals of conflict prevention and accountability.

The Potential of Blockchain and Digital Forensics in Preserving and Authenticating Evidence

Blockchain and digital forensics offer innovative solutions to ensure the integrity and reliability of evidence used in prosecutions. These technologies address longstanding challenges related to evidence preservation and authentication.

Blockchain for Evidence Integrity: Blockchain technology creates tamper-proof records of evidence, storing metadata such as timestamps, geolocation, and chain-of-custody details. This ensures that evidence remains unaltered from collection to presentation in court, significantly enhancing its credibility.

Digital Forensics: Forensic tools extract and authenticate data from devices like mobile phones, computers, and drones, frequently used in modern conflicts. Techniques such as metadata verification and image analysis meet the rigorous standards required for international prosecutions.

Open-Source Intelligence (OSINT): OSINT platforms aggregate publicly available data from social media, news outlets, and other sources, corroborating evidence and providing transparency. When combined with blockchain, OSINT offers verifiable and reliable documentation of violations, bridging gaps in traditional evidence collection methods.

Ethical and Legal Considerations in Using Technology for Justice

While AI and digital tools offer immense potential, their application in international justice raises critical ethical and legal concerns. Addressing these issues is essential to ensure their responsible and fair use.

Bias and Accuracy: AI algorithms may reflect biases present in the data they analyze, potentially leading to skewed findings. Ensuring diverse and representative datasets is crucial to maintaining fairness and accuracy in AI-driven processes.

Privacy and Surveillance: Evidence collection often involves sensitive personal information. Striking a balance between accountability and the protection of individuals' privacy rights is a key challenge in leveraging digital tools.

Admissibility in Court: Legal systems vary in their acceptance of AI-generated and digitally authenticated evidence. Establishing universal standards for admissibility ensures consistency and fairness in international prosecutions.

Accessibility and Equity: Advanced technologies often require significant resources, creating disparities between developed and less-developed nations. Democratizing access to these tools is essential to ensure global equity in justice processes.

Accountability for AI-Generated Evidence: Errors or inaccuracies in AI-generated evidence raise complex questions of accountability. Clear oversight mechanisms and guidelines are needed to prevent misuse and ensure transparency.

Thus, the incorporation of AI and digital tools into war crimes prosecution represents a pivotal advancement in the pursuit of international justice. These technologies enhance the efficiency and reliability of evidence analysis, strengthen the integrity of documentation, and offer innovative solutions to enduring challenges. However, their implementation must be guided by robust ethical and legal frameworks to ensure fairness, transparency, and respect for human rights.

As the chapter continues, the discussion will broaden to explore how collaboration among states, civil society, and technology can create a unified and resilient framework for addressing the complexities of modern conflicts. Together, innovation and collaboration offer a pathway to a more effective and equitable system of global justice.

10.4 Bridging Gaps: Collaboration Between States, Civil Society, and Technology

The pursuit of international justice is inherently a collective endeavor that hinges on the collaboration of states, civil society, and technological innovators. Governments and international institutions establish legal frameworks and mechanisms, while civil society plays a critical role in documenting atrocities, amplifying victims' voices, and advocating for justice. Meanwhile, technology enhances these efforts by offering tools for evidence collection, verification, and transparency. This section explores how partnerships among these stakeholders strengthen accountability, highlights civil society's role in bridging gaps, and underscores the importance of building trust in technology-driven justice processes.

Fostering Partnerships Between Governments and NGOs to Strengthen Accountability

Governments and non-governmental organizations (NGOs) bring complementary strengths to the justice process, each addressing different facets of accountability. Governments have the authority and resources to implement justice mechanisms, while NGOs possess the flexibility, local presence, and expertise to fill gaps in documentation and advocacy.

Collaborative Investigations: Partnerships between governments and NGOs enhance the thoroughness of investigations. NGOs with access to conflict zones can gather critical evidence and provide localized insights that inform state-led or international prosecutions.

Policy Influence and Advocacy: NGOs play a pivotal role in shaping accountability frameworks by identifying gaps and advocating for necessary reforms. Their research and recommendations guide governments in aligning national efforts with international standards.

Resource Sharing: Collaborative initiatives facilitate the pooling of resources, including funding, technical expertise, and personnel. For instance, joint projects between governments and NGOs in post-conflict societies have strengthened investigative capacities and accelerated accountability efforts.

Effective partnerships depend on clear communication, mutual respect, and shared objectives. By fostering these collaborations, governments and NGOs can establish more cohesive and efficient justice mechanisms.

Engaging Civil Society in Documenting and Advocating for Justice

Civil society organizations and grassroots movements serve as vital intermediaries between affected communities and formal justice systems. Their work extends beyond documentation to include advocacy, awareness-raising, and fostering trust in justice mechanisms.

Documenting Atrocities: Operating on the frontlines, civil society groups gather firsthand accounts, photographic evidence, and other critical materials. Their work complements formal investigations by uncovering hidden violations and providing localized perspectives.

Advocacy Campaigns: Civil society organizations mobilize public opinion through campaigns, petitions, and media outreach, exerting pressure on governments and international institutions to act. Global initiatives like **#JusticeForUkraine** demonstrate the power of grassroots efforts in shaping international discourse.

Empowering Victims: By ensuring victims' experiences and needs are central to justice processes, civil society fosters trust and inclusivity. Their advocacy creates platforms for victims to engage with justice mechanisms, reinforcing a victim-centered approach.

Building Trust in Technology-Driven Processes for War Crimes Prosecution

While technology has revolutionized the pursuit of justice, its effectiveness depends on the trust of stakeholders, including victims, witnesses, and the public. Ensuring transparency, ethical oversight, and inclusivity is critical to legitimizing technology-driven processes.

Transparency and Accountability: Clear guidelines on the use of technologies such as AI, blockchain, and digital forensics enhance public confidence. Transparent methodologies ensure that evidence collection and analysis remain credible and fair.

Training and Capacity Building: Providing training for investigators, civil society actors, and local authorities in using digital tools ensures consistent and accurate application. Empowering marginalized communities through capacity-building initiatives expands participation in justice processes.

Ethical Oversight: Establishing mechanisms for ethical oversight prevents the misuse of technology and safeguards privacy, human rights, and legal standards. These measures ensure that justice processes maintain their integrity and accountability.

Inclusive Design: Technology must be designed to be accessible and culturally sensitive, broadening participation in justice mechanisms. Collaborative development involving affected communities ensures that tools address specific needs effectively.

Thus, bridging gaps between states, civil society, and technology is essential for creating a unified and effective international justice system. Governments and NGOs bring complementary strengths to accountability efforts, while civil society amplifies victims' voices and ensures inclusivity. Technology enhances these processes, but its legitimacy relies on transparency, ethical oversight, and the meaningful involvement of all stakeholders.

As this chapter progresses, the discussion will turn to envisioning the future of global justice, focusing on lessons learned and strategies to create a resilient and adaptable system capable of addressing the complexities of modern conflicts. Through collaboration and innovation, the global community can pave the way for a more equitable and effective framework for justice.

10.5 A Vision for the Future: Toward a Resilient Global Justice System

The pursuit of international justice reflects humanity's enduring commitment to accountability, fairness, and the rule of law. However, the evolving nature of conflicts—shaped by technological advancements, non-state actors, and shifting geopolitical landscapes—demands a justice system that is resilient, inclusive, and adaptable. Building on the lessons of past efforts, this section outlines strategies for addressing emerging challenges, anticipates the future needs of global accountability, and envisions the elements of a sustainable framework for international justice.

Lessons Learned from Past Efforts in Shaping Future Justice Mechanisms

Decades of international justice initiatives, from the Nuremberg Trials to modern hybrid courts, provide invaluable lessons for shaping the future of accountability mechanisms. These insights highlight both successes and areas for growth:

Inclusivity as a Cornerstone: Effective justice mechanisms represent diverse voices, especially those of victims, marginalized communities, and underrepresented regions. Inclusivity strengthens trust and legitimacy, ensuring that justice reflects the collective will of the global community.

The Value of Collaboration: Initiatives such as hybrid courts and joint investigative teams demonstrate the importance of partnerships between international institutions, local actors, and civil society. Collaboration bridges gaps in resources and expertise, enhancing the overall effectiveness of justice processes.

Balancing Retributive and Restorative Approaches: While retributive justice focuses on accountability, integrating restorative elements such as reparations and truth-telling fosters healing and reconciliation. A balanced approach creates a holistic and lasting impact on affected communities.

Addressing Systemic Challenges: Shortcomings such as delays in prosecution, enforcement failures, and perceptions of bias have eroded trust in some institutions. Transparency, reform, and consistent application of justice principles are essential to restoring confidence in global mechanisms.

Anticipating Emerging Challenges in Global Accountability

The future of justice mechanisms must account for the dynamic nature of modern conflicts and the evolving global landscape. Key challenges include:

Technological Warfare: The rise of cyberattacks, autonomous weapons, and other forms of technological warfare introduces accountability gaps. Establishing clear legal frameworks to address these innovations is essential for maintaining global norms.

Non-State Actors: Many modern conflicts involve non-state entities such as terrorist groups, militias, and private military contractors. Expanding accountability mechanisms to address these actors will require innovative jurisdictional and legal solutions.

Geopolitical Polarization: Increasing division among global powers risks undermining international institutions. Strengthening multilateral cooperation and fostering neutrality in justice mechanisms can help mitigate these challenges.

Climate-Related Conflicts: As climate change exacerbates resource scarcity and displacement, new forms of conflict are emerging. Justice systems must adapt to address crimes arising from environmental factors, including violations of environmental rights.

Data Overload: The exponential growth of digital evidence presents both opportunities and challenges. Managing, authenticating, and analyzing vast datasets require advanced technological tools and universally accepted guidelines for admissibility.

Creating a Sustainable and Adaptable Framework for International Justice

To address these challenges, international justice systems must prioritize adaptability, inclusivity, and sustainability. Key elements of such a framework include:

Innovative Use of Technology: Leveraging AI, blockchain, and open-source intelligence enhances evidence collection, analysis, and preservation. Investments in technological infrastructure and training ensure that these tools are accessible to all nations.

Decentralized Justice Mechanisms: Expanding the role of regional courts and hybrid tribunals brings justice closer to affected communities, enhancing accessibility, cultural relevance, and efficiency. Decentralization also reduces dependence on overburdened international courts.

Strengthening Global Institutions: Reforms to institutions like the International Criminal Court (ICC) and United Nations (UN) should address biases, jurisdictional limitations, and enforcement challenges. Expanding membership, increasing funding, and improving transparency are critical steps toward more equitable and effective systems.

Promoting Preventative Justice: Incorporating early warning systems and real-time monitoring of human rights violations can help prevent conflicts before they escalate. Proactive approaches reduce the need for post-conflict accountability by addressing issues at their roots.

Institutionalizing Collaboration: Creating permanent platforms for collaboration between states, NGOs, civil society, and technology providers ensures that diverse perspectives and resources are integrated into justice efforts. Partnerships foster innovation and strengthen the resilience of accountability mechanisms.

Conclusion

A resilient global justice system must evolve to meet the complexities of modern conflicts while remaining rooted in the principles of accountability, fairness, and inclusivity. By learning from past successes and failures, anticipating future challenges, and embracing technological and structural innovation, the international community can create a sustainable framework capable of addressing the demands of an interconnected world.

As this chapter concludes, it leaves a hopeful call to action for global stakeholders to unite in their pursuit of justice. By fostering collaboration, transparency, and adaptability, the global justice system can ensure that no atrocity goes unpunished and no victim is forgotten, paving the way for a more just and equitable future.

Conclusion: Justice Beyond Borders

Justice, as a moral imperative, transcends geopolitical boundaries, embodying humanity's collective commitment to accountability and the rule of law. In an era marked by complex conflicts, the pursuit of justice faces unprecedented challenges, from technological advancements to entrenched political divisions. However, these obstacles underscore the necessity of a unified global response that aligns states, civil society, and technological innovation.

Reflections on Justice Amidst Geopolitical Tensions

The pursuit of justice in a world shaped by geopolitical tensions is an intricate endeavor, characterized by competing interests and conflicting priorities. As this book has explored, international mechanisms such as the International Criminal Court (ICC) and the United Nations (UN) are pivotal in addressing atrocities and holding perpetrators accountable. However, their efforts are often hampered by the realities of power dynamics, where the principles of justice clash with the interests of influential states. These tensions, while frustrating, underscore the importance of reform and innovation in the global justice system.

The Russia-Ukraine conflict serves as a contemporary case study of these challenges. On one hand, the ICC has launched investigations and issued arrest warrants to address alleged war crimes, highlighting the court's dedication to accountability. On the other hand, Russia's status as a permanent member of the UN Security Council with veto power has paralyzed broader international responses. This juxtaposition reveals the structural vulnerabilities within current mechanisms: institutions designed to uphold justice are often constrained by the very powers they seek to regulate.

Similar patterns emerge in other conflicts where geopolitics overshadow justice. From the gridlock in addressing the Syrian civil war to the selective enforcement of international law, these examples illustrate how political alliances and economic dependencies can undermine accountability. Yet, these challenges do not negate the moral and legal imperative to act. Instead, they demand a reimagining of international justice systems—one that prioritizes equity, inclusivity, and resilience over the entrenched biases of existing frameworks.

Historical precedents offer both cautionary tales and sources of inspiration. The Nuremberg Trials, established in the aftermath of World War II, were not without controversy; critics questioned their legitimacy, labeling them as "victor's justice." Despite these criticisms, Nuremberg set enduring legal and moral precedents, introducing the principle of individual accountability and defining crimes against humanity. Similarly, the International Criminal Tribunal for the former Yugoslavia (ICTY) faced logistical and political hurdles, yet it demonstrated the international community's resolve to address atrocities and contribute to reconciliation.

These historical frameworks highlight an essential truth: justice mechanisms are imperfect but adaptable. Their evolution reflects humanity's capacity to learn, persevere, and refine its approaches in response to emerging challenges. While geopolitics often hinder immediate progress, they also emphasize the necessity of building systems that are insulated from undue influence and capable of enduring political pressures.

The path forward requires reforms that strengthen the autonomy and legitimacy of global justice institutions. This involves limiting the use of veto power in cases of mass atrocities, broadening representation to include underrepresented regions, and enhancing enforcement mechanisms to ensure that rulings are upheld. Moreover, fostering global solidarity—through multilateral diplomacy, civil society advocacy, and technological innovation—can help counterbalance the weight of geopolitical tensions.

In reflecting on justice amidst these tensions, it becomes clear that the pursuit of accountability is not merely a legal exercise but a moral endeavor. It reaffirms humanity's collective commitment to fairness, dignity, and the rule of law. While the road ahead is fraught with challenges, the lessons of the past and the potential of innovation provide hope that justice can prevail, even in the most polarized and contentious of times.

A Call for Global Solidarity

Global solidarity in the face of injustice is not merely an ideal; it is a profound necessity, a moral imperative that binds humanity together in its shared commitment to fairness and accountability. Injustice anywhere resonates everywhere, threatening the very fabric of global stability and peace. To confront this challenge, we must embrace the collective strength of civil society movements, investigative journalism, and technological innovation—forces that amplify the voices of victims, uncover hidden truths, and hold perpetrators to account. Yet, these efforts cannot succeed in isolation; they demand unwavering collaboration among governments, NGOs, international institutions, and innovators to create systems that are not only efficient but also ethical.

The task is daunting. It requires the courage to confront power, the resolve to reform entrenched institutions, and the humility to recognize the limitations of past efforts. However, the alternative—indifference, inaction, or acceptance of impunity—is far more costly. By addressing systemic flaws, embracing inclusivity, and leveraging the transformative potential of technology, humanity can create a justice system that transcends borders and barriers, one that reflects the universal values of equity, dignity, and accountability.

As this book concludes, it leaves a hopeful call to action: to reinforce international justice as a cornerstone of global governance. This is not a responsibility that rests solely with institutions or leaders; it is a shared duty, one that requires a collective moral commitment to uphold the principles that define our humanity. Justice must not be confined by geography or politics; it must serve as a beacon for all, a reminder that the sanctity of human life and the rule of law are principles worth defending at any cost.

The pursuit of justice beyond borders is not merely a legal undertaking; it is a testament to our enduring belief in the dignity of life. It is an acknowledgment that while the scars of conflict run deep, the resilience of the human spirit runs deeper. Justice is not an end in itself but a bridge to reconciliation, healing, and peace—a path forward for societies fractured by violence and division.

As we look to the future, let this call for solidarity inspire action. Let it remind us that the pursuit of justice is not a solitary endeavor but a shared journey. It is a journey that demands courage in the face of adversity, compassion for those who suffer, and an unyielding commitment to the principles that unite us as a global community.

Let this be the foundation upon which future generations build a world that is not only more equitable and just but also more empathetic and united. Together, in solidarity, we can ensure that no atrocity goes unpunished, no victim is forgotten, and no voice is silenced. Let us leave a legacy of justice that transcends borders and generations—a legacy that reaffirms our shared humanity and our collective capacity to shape a more peaceful and compassionate world.

Appendices

Appendix 1: Key International Legal Frameworks

The pursuit of international justice is anchored in a robust foundation of treaties, statutes, and conventions that establish the principles and mechanisms for addressing war crimes, crimes against humanity, and genocide. This appendix summarizes the key legal frameworks that underpin global accountability efforts and serve as benchmarks for justice systems worldwide.

1. The Rome Statute (1998)

The Rome Statute is the foundational treaty of the International Criminal Court (ICC), adopted in 1998 and entering into force in 2002. It provides the legal framework for prosecuting individuals responsible for genocide, war crimes, crimes against humanity, and the crime of aggression.

Key Provisions:

✓ Establishes the ICC as a permanent international tribunal.

✓ Operates on the principle of complementarity, intervening only when national judicial systems are unable or unwilling to prosecute.

✓ Defines core international crimes and the conditions for their prosecution.

Significance: The Rome Statute represents a landmark in international law, providing a global mechanism for accountability. However, its jurisdiction is limited to member states or cases referred by the UN Security Council, highlighting the need for broader ratification and enforcement.

2. The Geneva Conventions (1949)

The Geneva Conventions, adopted in the aftermath of World War II, are a cornerstone of international humanitarian law. Comprising four treaties and three additional protocols, they set the standards for humane treatment during armed conflict.

Key Provisions:

✓ Protection of wounded and sick soldiers on land and at sea.

✓ Humane treatment of prisoners of war.

✓ Safeguarding civilians in conflict zones.

✓ Prohibition of acts such as torture, collective punishment, and targeting non-combatants.

Significance: Ratified by virtually every nation, the Geneva Conventions provide a universal framework for limiting the suffering caused by war. They remain essential for assessing violations and prosecuting war crimes.

3. The Universal Declaration of Human Rights (1948)

Adopted by the United Nations General Assembly, the Universal Declaration of Human Rights (UDHR) is a foundational document that outlines the inherent rights and freedoms of all individuals.

Key Provisions:

✓ Affirms the right to life, liberty, and security of person.
✓ Prohibits slavery, torture, and inhumane treatment.
✓ Recognizes equality before the law and the right to a fair trial.
✓ Guarantees freedom of thought, expression, and assembly.

Significance: While not legally binding, the UDHR has inspired numerous international treaties and national constitutions. It provides the moral and legal basis for human rights advocacy and accountability efforts globally.

4. The Genocide Convention (1948)

The Convention on the Prevention and Punishment of the Crime of Genocide, commonly known as the Genocide Convention, was the first human rights treaty adopted by the UN. It defines genocide and establishes the obligation to prevent and punish this crime.

Key Provisions:

✓ Defines genocide as acts committed with the intent to destroy, in whole or in part, a national, ethnic, racial, or religious group.

✓ Mandates states to enact laws to prevent and punish genocide.

✓ Provides the basis for international and national prosecution of genocide.

Significance:

The Genocide Convention laid the groundwork for prosecuting atrocities such as the Holocaust, the Rwandan Genocide, and the Bosnian Genocide. It underscores the international community's commitment to preventing the gravest crimes against humanity.

5. Regional Frameworks

Regional legal frameworks complement international efforts by addressing specific geopolitical and cultural contexts. These frameworks often enhance the reach and relevance of global accountability mechanisms.

Examples:

African Charter on Human and Peoples' Rights (1981): Protects human rights and promotes accountability across Africa, with the African Court on Human and Peoples' Rights providing judicial oversight.

European Convention on Human Rights (1950): Ensures the protection of civil and political rights in Europe, enforced by the European Court of Human Rights.

Inter-American Convention on Human Rights (1969): Safeguards human rights in the Americas, adjudicated by the Inter-American Court of Human Rights.

Significance: Regional frameworks provide localized mechanisms for addressing human rights violations and war crimes. They complement international treaties by reflecting the unique challenges and priorities of their respective regions.

Conclusion

These foundational legal frameworks represent humanity's collective resolve to uphold justice, dignity, and the rule of law. Together, they form the bedrock of international accountability mechanisms, guiding efforts to address atrocities and protect fundamental human rights. As the global landscape evolves, these frameworks must continue to adapt, ensuring their relevance and effectiveness in the pursuit of justice.

Appendix 2: Glossary of Terms

This glossary provides definitions for key terms used throughout the book, offering clarity on the concepts and mechanisms that underpin international justice and accountability.

War Crimes

Acts committed during armed conflict that violate international humanitarian law, such as willful killing, torture, taking hostages, targeting civilians, or using prohibited weapons. War crimes are addressed under frameworks like the Geneva Conventions and the Rome Statute.

Crimes Against Humanity

Widespread or systematic attacks directed against civilian populations, such as murder, enslavement, deportation, torture, and persecution. Unlike war crimes, crimes against humanity can occur during peacetime and are defined under the Rome Statute.

Genocide

The intentional destruction, in whole or in part, of a national, ethnic, racial, or religious group. Genocide involves acts such as killing members of the group, causing serious harm, or forcibly transferring children, and is defined by the Genocide Convention.

Restorative Justice

A justice approach that focuses on repairing harm and restoring relationships rather than punishment. It involves dialogue, acknowledgment of wrongdoing, and measures to address victims' needs, contributing to reconciliation and societal healing.

Hybrid Courts

Courts that combine international and domestic legal principles, personnel, and jurisdiction to address specific conflicts. Hybrid courts, such as the Extraordinary Chambers in the Courts of Cambodia, balance global expertise with local context to deliver justice.

Universal Jurisdiction

A legal principle allowing states to prosecute serious crimes like genocide, war crimes, and crimes against humanity, regardless of where they were committed or the nationality of the perpetrators or victims. Universal jurisdiction aims to prevent impunity for the gravest offenses.

Open-Source Intelligence (OSINT)

Information collected from publicly available sources, such as social media, news outlets, and online platforms, used in investigations and evidence collection. OSINT plays a crucial role in documenting war crimes and corroborating other forms of evidence.

Conclusion

These terms represent the foundational concepts of international justice and are integral to understanding the pursuit of accountability in the face of modern conflicts and atrocities. This glossary serves as a quick reference for readers to navigate the complex and evolving landscape of global justice.

Appendix 3: Case Studies Summary

This appendix offers concise summaries of the major case studies explored throughout the book, highlighting their significance in shaping the pursuit of international justice and accountability.

Nuremberg Trials (1945-1946)

The Nuremberg Trials marked the first international tribunal to hold individuals accountable for crimes committed during World War II, particularly those orchestrated by Nazi Germany. The trials established key legal principles, including individual accountability for state-led atrocities, the rejection of the "following orders" defense, and the codification of crimes against humanity. Conducted by the Allied powers, the trials set enduring precedents for international justice, forming the foundation for subsequent frameworks like the ICC and Geneva Conventions.

ICTY: International Criminal Tribunal for the Former Yugoslavia (1993-2017)

The ICTY was established by the United Nations to address war crimes, crimes against humanity, and genocide committed during the violent breakup of Yugoslavia in the 1990s. Key milestones included the prosecution of high-profile leaders like Slobodan Milošević and Ratko Mladić, who were held accountable for atrocities, including the Srebrenica massacre. Despite challenges such as political resistance and lengthy trials, the ICTY demonstrated the potential of international justice to address regional conflicts and contributed to the development of modern accountability mechanisms.

ICTR: International Criminal Tribunal for Rwanda (1994-2015)

Created in response to the 1994 genocide in Rwanda, which claimed the lives of approximately 800,000 people, the ICTR prosecuted key figures responsible for orchestrating the atrocities. Landmark cases included the conviction of former Prime Minister Jean Kambanda for genocide. The ICTR expanded the legal definitions of crimes against humanity, particularly recognizing sexual violence as a tool of genocide. Its work emphasized the importance of balancing justice with reconciliation in post-conflict societies.

Truth and Reconciliation Commissions (South Africa and Sierra Leone)

Truth and Reconciliation Commissions (TRCs) provide non-judicial platforms for confronting past atrocities and fostering national healing.

South Africa's TRC (1996-2002): This commission addressed apartheid-era crimes by allowing perpetrators to seek amnesty in exchange for full disclosure. Its emphasis on acknowledgment and forgiveness enabled South Africa to transition toward democracy and unity.

Sierra Leone's TRC (2002-2004): Following a decade-long civil war, Sierra Leone's TRC gave marginalized groups, including women and children, a platform to share their experiences. By documenting the conflict's systemic patterns of violence, the TRC contributed to rebuilding trust and social cohesion.

Modern Conflicts: Russia-Ukraine, Syria, and Myanmar

Modern conflicts reveal the evolving challenges of international justice, including geopolitical tensions, technological complexities, and non-state actors.

Russia-Ukraine: The ongoing conflict has brought allegations of war crimes, including civilian targeting and forced deportations. Investigations by the ICC and global advocacy campaigns highlight the need for real-time documentation and accountability amidst active hostilities.

Syria: The Syrian civil war has been marked by chemical weapon attacks, targeting of civilians, and widespread displacement. Despite overwhelming evidence, accountability efforts face obstacles due to geopolitical divisions within the UN Security Council.

Myanmar: The persecution of the Rohingya people has been described as genocide by international observers. Efforts to hold Myanmar's military accountable are ongoing, with the ICC and civil society organizations documenting crimes and advocating for justice.

Conclusion

These case studies illuminate the evolution of international justice mechanisms, from groundbreaking historical tribunals to ongoing challenges in modern conflicts. They underscore the importance of adapting legal frameworks, fostering collaboration, and addressing systemic barriers to ensure accountability and justice in an increasingly complex world.

Appendix 4: Timeline of International Justice

This timeline highlights significant milestones in the evolution of international justice, illustrating humanity's ongoing commitment to accountability and the rule of law.

1945-1946: Establishment of the Nuremberg Trials

The first international tribunal to hold individuals accountable for war crimes, crimes against humanity, and genocide committed during World War II.

Key figures from Nazi Germany were prosecuted, establishing the principle of individual accountability for state-led atrocities.

1948: Adoption of the Genocide Convention

The United Nations adopted the Convention on the Prevention and Punishment of the Crime of Genocide, defining genocide as a crime under international law and obligating states to prevent and punish it.

1949: Ratification of the Geneva Conventions

Four treaties were ratified, setting universal standards for humanitarian treatment during armed conflicts, including protections for civilians, prisoners of war, and medical personnel.

1993: Establishment of the ICTY

The International Criminal Tribunal for the former Yugoslavia was created by the United Nations to address atrocities committed during the Balkan conflicts.

Delivered landmark verdicts, including the conviction of Radovan Karadžić for genocide and war crimes.

1994: Establishment of the ICTR

Created in response to the Rwandan Genocide, the ICTR prosecuted key figures responsible for orchestrating mass killings, including Jean Kambanda, the first head of government convicted of genocide.

2002: Creation of the International Criminal Court (ICC)

The Rome Statute entered into force, establishing the ICC as a permanent international tribunal to prosecute genocide, war crimes, crimes against humanity, and the crime of aggression.

The ICC operates on the principle of complementarity, intervening when national systems are unable or unwilling to act.

2005: Establishment of the Special Court for Sierra Leone

A hybrid court combining international and domestic elements to prosecute crimes committed during Sierra Leone's civil war.

Secured the conviction of Charles Taylor, the former President of Liberia, for aiding and abetting war crimes.

2017: Conclusion of the ICTY

The ICTY completed its mandate after issuing 161 indictments and delivering groundbreaking judgments that advanced the field of international law.

The tribunal set legal precedents on genocide, sexual violence, and command responsibility.

2018: ICC Investigation into Myanmar

The ICC initiated investigations into the alleged genocide of the Rohingya people, marking one of its most significant cases addressing crimes committed by state and military actors.

2022: Investigations into Russia-Ukraine War Crimes

The ICC launched investigations into allegations of war crimes, crimes against humanity, and forced deportations during the Russia-Ukraine conflict.

The international community mobilized efforts to document and address atrocities in real-time.

Conclusion

This timeline reflects the evolution of international justice, from the foundational Nuremberg Trials to contemporary efforts in addressing modern conflicts. Each milestone represents a step forward in the pursuit of accountability and underscores the need for continued innovation and collaboration to uphold the principles of fairness and human dignity in an ever-changing global landscape.

Appendix 5: Tools and Technologies in Justice

The advancement of technology has transformed the field of international justice, providing innovative tools that enhance evidence collection, analysis, and verification. This appendix explores key technologies discussed in the book, highlighting their applications in addressing the complexities of modern conflicts.

Artificial Intelligence (AI) in Evidence Analysis

AI has become an indispensable tool in managing and analyzing the vast volumes of evidence generated during conflicts. Its ability to process data efficiently and identify patterns has revolutionized case building and investigations.

Applications:

Pattern Recognition: AI algorithms analyze satellite imagery, videos, and social media content to detect systematic violations, such as troop movements or deliberate attacks on civilians.

Automated Sorting: AI categorizes digital evidence based on relevance and reliability, reducing the workload on investigators and expediting justice processes.

Natural Language Processing (NLP): NLP tools process multilingual documents, interviews, and transcripts, identifying key themes and connections in complex cases.

Predictive Analysis: AI predicts potential violations by analyzing historical data and real-time inputs, enabling preventive measures and rapid responses.

Significance:

AI enhances the efficiency, accuracy, and scalability of evidence analysis, allowing justice mechanisms to address large-scale conflicts with precision and speed.

Blockchain for Evidence Preservation

Blockchain technology provides a secure and transparent method for preserving evidence, ensuring its integrity from collection to presentation in court. Its tamper-proof nature makes it a valuable tool for maintaining the credibility of digital materials.

Applications:

Chain of Custody: Blockchain creates an immutable record of evidence, including timestamps, geolocation, and chain-of-custody details, ensuring that materials remain unaltered.

Transparency: Courts, investigators, and stakeholders can access a verifiable history of how evidence was handled, reducing disputes over its authenticity.

Global Collaboration: Blockchain facilitates seamless sharing of evidence across jurisdictions, enabling collaborative investigations while maintaining data security.

Significance:

By safeguarding evidence integrity, blockchain addresses challenges related to tampering and mistrust, reinforcing the reliability of international justice processes.

Digital Forensics and Metadata Verification

Digital forensics involves extracting and authenticating data from devices such as smartphones, computers, and drones, which are increasingly used in modern conflicts. Metadata verification ensures that digital evidence meets legal standards for authenticity.

Applications:

Data Extraction: Forensic tools retrieve deleted files, communications, and other data critical to investigations.

Metadata Analysis: Techniques verify the origin, timestamps, and geolocation of photos, videos, and documents, ensuring their credibility in court.

Device Analysis: Investigators analyze devices used by perpetrators to uncover patterns of communication, planning, and execution of crimes.

Significance:

Digital forensics bridges the gap between digital and physical evidence, providing robust documentation that withstands legal scrutiny.

Open-Source Intelligence (OSINT) Platforms

OSINT platforms, such as **Bellingcat**, aggregate publicly available data from social media, news outlets, and online resources to support investigations and corroborate evidence.

Applications:

Conflict Monitoring: OSINT aggregates real-time data from conflict zones, documenting violations as they occur.

Corroborating Evidence: Platforms validate claims using geolocation, timestamps, and cross-referencing with other sources.

Transparency: By utilizing publicly available data, OSINT fosters trust and accessibility in justice processes.

Significance:

OSINT democratizes evidence collection, enabling civil society, journalists, and investigators to contribute to justice efforts and uncover hidden truths.

Conclusion

The integration of AI, blockchain, digital forensics, and OSINT into international justice mechanisms represents a paradigm shift in how war crimes and atrocities are documented and prosecuted. These technologies enhance efficiency, credibility, and inclusivity, addressing many of the challenges posed by modern conflicts. However, their application must be guided by ethical considerations and robust legal frameworks to ensure fairness and transparency. Together, these tools offer a transformative pathway for advancing accountability and upholding the principles of justice in an increasingly complex global landscape.

Appendix 6: Resources for Further Reading

To deepen your understanding of the themes explored in this book, the following resources provide valuable insights into international justice, accountability, reconciliation, and the role of technology in modern conflicts. These books, articles, reports, and websites offer a comprehensive starting point for further exploration.

Key Publications on International Law and Justice

"International Law" by Malcolm Shaw

A definitive guide to the principles and frameworks of international law, including sections on humanitarian law and accountability mechanisms.

"The Nuremberg Trials: The Nazis and Their Crimes Against Humanity" by Paul Roland

A detailed examination of the Nuremberg Trials and their impact on the development of international justice.

"The International Criminal Court: A Global Civilizing Force?" by Phil Clark

Analyzes the ICC's role, successes, and challenges in addressing global accountability.

"Human Rights: A Very Short Introduction" by Andrew Clapham

An accessible overview of human rights principles and their intersection with global justice.

"Restorative Justice: Ideas, Values, Debates" by Gerry Johnstone

Explores the philosophy and application of restorative justice in post-conflict societies.

Reports from the ICC, UN, and Other Global Bodies

International Criminal Court Annual Reports

Available on the official ICC website, these reports detail ongoing cases, investigations, and the court's operational challenges.

Website: www.icc-cpi.int[1]

1. https://www.icc-cpi.int

United Nations Human Rights Reports

Covers global human rights violations, including investigations into war crimes and atrocities.

Website: www.ohchr.org[2]

Global Centre for the Responsibility to Protect Reports

Focuses on preventing genocide, war crimes, and crimes against humanity.

Website: www.globalr2p.org[3]

Amnesty International and Human Rights Watch Reports

Document violations of international law and advocate for accountability in conflicts such as Syria, Myanmar, and Ukraine.

Websites: www.amnesty.org[4] and www.hrw.org[5]

Research Papers on Restorative Justice, Reconciliation, and Modern Conflicts

"Restorative Justice in Post-Conflict Societies" by Thalia González

Explores the application of restorative justice in transitional settings, emphasizing its role in reconciliation and societal healing.

"Reconciliation and Justice: The Role of Truth Commissions" by Priscilla B. Hayner

Analyzes the effectiveness of truth commissions in addressing past atrocities and fostering peace.

"Hybrid Courts and International Justice" by Laura A. Dickinson

Examines the role of hybrid courts in bridging global standards with local contexts for effective justice.

"The Impact of Technology on War Crimes Investigations" by Alexa Koenig

Discusses the transformative role of AI, blockchain, and digital forensics in modern accountability efforts.

"Geopolitical Challenges in International Justice" by Mark Kersten

Addresses the intersection of political power and accountability mechanisms in the global justice system.

2. https://www.ohchr.org
3. https://www.globalr2p.org
4. https://www.amnesty.org
5. https://www.hrw.org

Websites and Online Platforms

International Justice Resource Center

Provides in-depth resources on human rights and accountability mechanisms.

Website: www.ijrcenter.org[6]

Bellingcat

A leading open-source intelligence platform known for its investigations into war crimes and human rights violations.

Website: www.bellingcat.com[7]

The Global Justice Center

Focuses on gender equality and the rule of law in conflict and post-conflict settings.

Website: www.globaljusticecenter.net[8]

The International Crisis Group

Offers analysis and recommendations for preventing and resolving deadly conflicts.

Website: www.crisisgroup.org[9]

Truth Commissions Digital Collection (University of Wisconsin)

A repository of reports and documents from truth commissions around the world.

Website: www.law.wisc.edu/gls/truthcom.htm

Conclusion

These resources provide a wealth of information for readers seeking to deepen their knowledge of international justice, restorative practices, and the evolving challenges of addressing modern conflicts. They complement the themes of this book and serve as a guide for those committed to understanding and advancing the principles of accountability and human dignity.

6. https://www.ijrcenter.org
7. https://www.bellingcat.com
8. https://www.globaljusticecenter.net
9. https://www.crisisgroup.org

Appendix 7: Profiles of Major International Institutions

This appendix provides an overview of the institutions that play a critical role in the pursuit of global justice. From legal tribunals to advocacy organizations, these entities form the backbone of international efforts to uphold accountability, protect human rights, and address atrocities.

1. The International Criminal Court (ICC)

Overview: Established in 2002 under the Rome Statute, the ICC is the first permanent international tribunal dedicated to prosecuting genocide, war crimes, crimes against humanity, and the crime of aggression.

Mandate: The ICC intervenes when national judicial systems are unable or unwilling to prosecute serious international crimes. Operating on the principle of complementarity, it supplements national efforts rather than replacing them.

Jurisdiction: Limited to crimes committed in the territories of member states or referred by the UN Security Council. Non-signatory states, such as the United States, Russia, and China, are outside its jurisdiction unless they accept the court's authority for specific cases.

Notable Cases: The prosecution of Thomas Lubanga (recruitment of child soldiers) and the arrest warrant for Omar al-Bashir (genocide in Darfur).

Challenges: The ICC faces criticism for selective justice, enforcement limitations, and political resistance, particularly from non-member states.

2. United Nations Security Council (UNSC)

Overview: One of the six principal organs of the United Nations, the UNSC is charged with maintaining international peace and security. It has the authority to establish tribunals, impose sanctions, and authorize military interventions.

Structure: Composed of 15 members: five permanent members (United States, Russia, China, United Kingdom, and France) with veto power, and 10 rotating members elected for two-year terms.

Role in Justice: The UNSC has referred cases to the ICC, such as Darfur (2005) and Libya (2011). It also established ad hoc tribunals like the ICTY and ICTR to address specific conflicts.

Criticism: The veto power of permanent members often leads to gridlock, preventing decisive action in cases like the Syrian civil war and the Russia-Ukraine conflict.

3. Regional Courts

Overview: Regional courts provide localized mechanisms for addressing human rights violations and promoting accountability, often complementing global efforts.

Examples:

African Court on Human and Peoples' Rights (ACHPR): Established in 2006, the ACHPR safeguards human rights across Africa, interpreting the African Charter on Human and Peoples' Rights.

European Court of Human Rights (ECHR): Oversees the implementation of the European Convention on Human Rights, addressing violations within Council of Europe member states.

Inter-American Court of Human Rights (IACHR): Adjudicates cases related to the American Convention on Human Rights in the Americas.

Significance: Regional courts address specific cultural and geopolitical contexts, providing accessible and culturally sensitive justice mechanisms.

4. Truth and Reconciliation Commissions (TRCs)

Overview: TRCs are non-judicial bodies designed to uncover the truth about past human rights violations and promote reconciliation in post-conflict societies.

Role: Documenting systemic patterns of violence and human rights abuses.

Providing victims with a platform to share their experiences and receive acknowledgment.

Recommending measures for reparations, institutional reforms, and social healing.

Examples:

South Africa's TRC: Addressed apartheid-era crimes, combining truth-telling with amnesty for full disclosure.

Sierra Leone's TRC: Focused on addressing the impacts of the civil war, with a special emphasis on marginalized groups such as women and children.

Impact: TRCs foster societal healing and collective understanding, often working alongside judicial mechanisms like hybrid courts.

5. Non-Governmental Organizations (NGOs)

Overview: NGOs play a critical role in advocating for justice, documenting violations, and supporting victims. Their flexibility and localized presence allow them to address gaps in formal justice mechanisms.

Examples:

Amnesty International: Focuses on human rights advocacy, publishing reports on violations and pressuring governments to act.

Human Rights Watch (HRW): Conducts investigations and reports on human rights abuses, influencing international discourse and policy.

Role in Justice: Documenting evidence of atrocities in conflict zones.

Mobilizing public opinion through advocacy campaigns.

Providing legal and psychological support to victims.

Challenges: NGOs often operate in hostile environments, facing threats from governments and non-state actors resistant to accountability.

Conclusion

These institutions collectively form the infrastructure of international justice, each playing a unique role in addressing atrocities and promoting accountability. From the legal authority of the ICC and regional courts to the advocacy and documentation efforts of NGOs and TRCs, these entities demonstrate the power of collaboration in pursuing a just and equitable world. By understanding their contributions and challenges, we can appreciate the multifaceted nature of global justice and the ongoing need for innovation and reform.

Appendix 8: Victim-Centric Advocacy Resources

This appendix provides essential resources for victims and survivors of war crimes and atrocities. These resources include organizations that offer support, contact information for key international and regional justice bodies, and guidance on accessing reparations and legal assistance.

Organizations Supporting Victims of War Crimes and Atrocities

Amnesty International

✓ **Focus:** Advocacy for human rights and justice, including support for victims of war crimes.

✓ **Services:** Documentation of violations, advocacy campaigns, and pressure on governments to deliver justice.

✓ **Website:** www.amnesty.org[10]

Human Rights Watch (HRW)

✓ **Focus:** Investigating and exposing human rights abuses globally.

✓ **Services:** Reports on atrocities, advocacy for accountability, and support for victims through awareness campaigns.

✓ **Website:** www.hrw.org[11]

International Committee of the Red Cross (ICRC)

✓ **Focus:** Protecting victims of armed conflict and providing humanitarian aid.

10. https://www.amnesty.org

11. https://www.hrw.org

✓ **Services:** Reunification of families, psychological support, and legal assistance for survivors.

✓ **Website:** www.icrc.org[12]

Global Survivors Fund

✓ **Focus:** Supporting survivors of conflict-related sexual violence.

✓ **Services:** Access to reparations, advocacy, and financial assistance for victims.

✓ **Website:** www.globalsurvivorsfund.org[13]

Coalition for the International Criminal Court (CICC)

✓ **Focus:** Advocacy for the ICC and support for victims engaged in international justice processes.

✓ **Services:** Legal guidance, awareness campaigns, and connection to local organizations.

✓ **Website:** www.coalitionfortheicc.org[14]

Contact Information for International and Regional Justice Bodies

International Criminal Court (ICC)

✓ **Contact:** Office of the Prosecutor
✓ Email: otp.informationdesk@icc-cpi.int
✓ Website: www.icc-cpi.int[15]

12. https://www.icrc.org

13. https://www.globalsurvivorsfund.org

14. https://www.coalitionfortheicc.org

15. https://www.icc-cpi.int

African Court on Human and Peoples' Rights (ACHPR)

✓ **Contact:** Email: registrar@african-court.org
✓ Website: www.african-court.org[16]

European Court of Human Rights (ECHR)

✓ **Contact:** Email: echr@echr.coe.int
✓ Website: www.echr.coe.int

Inter-American Court of Human Rights (IACHR)

✓ **Contact:** Email: corteidh@corteidh.or.cr
✓ Website: www.corteidh.or.cr

United Nations Office of the High Commissioner for Human Rights (OHCHR)

✓ **Contact:** Email: infodesk@ohchr.org
✓ Website: www.ohchr.org[17]

Guides on Accessing Reparations and Legal Assistance

Accessing Reparations

Step 1: Identify applicable reparations programs (e.g., national governments, international courts, or specialized funds like the Global Survivors Fund).

Step 2: Submit documentation of harm suffered, including evidence of losses and testimonials.

Step 3: Engage with local or international advocacy organizations for guidance and assistance during the application process.

Seeking Legal Assistance

16. https://www.african-court.org

17. https://www.ohchr.org

Step 1: Contact regional or international justice bodies to understand available legal avenues.

Step 2: Connect with NGOs or legal aid organizations specializing in human rights and war crimes.

Step 3: Gather evidence, testimonies, and documentation with the help of legal professionals or investigators.

Additional Support Services

Trauma Counseling: Many organizations, such as the ICRC and national human rights commissions, offer psychological support to victims.

Community Support Programs: Engage with local initiatives for group counseling and peer support, fostering collective healing.

Conclusion

Victims and survivors are at the heart of international justice, and their voices must be heard and their needs addressed. The resources listed here provide pathways for victims to seek reparations, legal assistance, and emotional support. By empowering survivors and amplifying their stories, these organizations and institutions contribute to a more just and compassionate world.

Appendix 9: Ethical Guidelines for Using Technology in Justice

As technology becomes an integral part of justice mechanisms, it is essential to establish ethical guidelines to ensure its responsible and effective use. Leveraging tools like AI, blockchain, and digital forensics offers immense potential to enhance accountability and transparency. However, these advancements must be implemented with safeguards that protect individual rights and uphold the principles of fairness and equity.

Privacy Safeguards

The collection and analysis of digital evidence often involve handling sensitive personal information. Safeguarding the privacy of victims, witnesses, and affected communities is paramount to maintaining trust in technology-driven justice processes.

Data Protection: All evidence must be stored and processed in compliance with international data protection standards, such as the GDPR. This includes encrypting sensitive information and restricting access to authorized personnel only.

Informed Consent: Individuals whose data is collected must be informed about its purpose, use, and storage. Seeking consent ensures that victims and witnesses are aware of and agree to their involvement in justice processes.

Minimizing Data Collection: Only the data necessary for specific investigations should be collected to reduce the risk of misuse or exposure.

Anonymization and Pseudonymization: Anonymizing data where possible, especially in public records or reports, protects the identities of victims and witnesses while allowing evidence to be used effectively.

Avoiding Bias in AI Algorithms

AI algorithms can inadvertently reflect and perpetuate biases present in the data they analyze. Ensuring that AI applications in justice are impartial and reliable requires proactive measures.

Representative Training Data: AI systems should be trained on diverse and balanced datasets that accurately reflect the context of conflicts and avoid reinforcing stereotypes or prejudices.

Regular Audits: Conducting periodic audits of AI tools helps identify and address biases in their operation, ensuring fairness and accuracy in evidence analysis and decision-making.

Human Oversight: AI-driven insights should complement, not replace, human judgment. Investigators and legal professionals must critically evaluate AI outputs and contextualize them within broader evidence.

Accountability for Bias: Clear guidelines on accountability for biases in AI systems ensure that developers, implementers, and users take responsibility for their impacts.

Ensuring Transparency and Accountability

Transparency in how technology is used in justice processes fosters trust among stakeholders, including victims, witnesses, and the broader public. Accountability mechanisms ensure that tools are applied ethically and effectively.

Documentation of Processes: All steps involving digital tools, from evidence collection to analysis, must be thoroughly documented to provide a clear chain of custody and ensure procedural integrity.

Open Standards: Adopting open-source technologies and methodologies promotes transparency, allowing independent experts to validate the processes and results.

Public Communication: Clearly communicating the role and limitations of technology in investigations and prosecutions helps manage expectations and build confidence in justice mechanisms.

Oversight Committees: Establishing independent oversight bodies ensures that technology is used in accordance with ethical and legal standards. These committees can evaluate the impact of tools on justice processes and recommend improvements.

Conclusion

The integration of technology into justice mechanisms presents a unique opportunity to enhance accountability and efficiency. However, its responsible use requires adherence to strict ethical guidelines. By prioritizing privacy safeguards, mitigating biases in AI algorithms, and ensuring transparency and accountability, stakeholders can harness the power of technology while protecting the rights and dignity of those affected by conflict. These practices will reinforce trust in digital tools as an essential component of modern justice.

Appendix 10: Reflection Questions

To deepen engagement with the themes explored in this book, the following reflection questions encourage readers to critically examine the challenges, opportunities, and complexities of international justice. These questions are designed to provoke thoughtful discussion, inspire new perspectives, and foster a deeper understanding of global accountability mechanisms.

1. How Can Global Justice Systems Balance Sovereignty and Accountability?

1. What are the key challenges in reconciling state sovereignty with the need for international oversight in cases of war crimes and atrocities?
2. How can justice mechanisms respect national jurisdiction while ensuring that perpetrators of international crimes are held accountable?
3. Should sovereignty ever be compromised for the sake of justice? If so, under what circumstances?
4. What reforms could be implemented to make global justice systems more effective while respecting the principles of sovereignty?

2. What Role Does Civil Society Play in Shaping Justice Mechanisms?

1. How do civil society organizations complement the work of international institutions like the ICC and regional courts?
2. In what ways can grassroots movements and NGOs amplify the voices of victims and marginalized groups in justice processes?
3. What challenges do civil society organizations face in documenting atrocities and advocating for accountability?
4. How can governments and international bodies better collaborate with civil society to strengthen justice mechanisms?

3. How Can Technology Be Harnessed Ethically to Advance Justice?

1. What are the most promising applications of AI, blockchain, and digital tools in war crimes documentation and prosecution?

2. How can we ensure that these technologies are used responsibly and without infringing on privacy or human rights?
3. What measures can be taken to address biases in AI algorithms and ensure equitable access to digital tools for less-resourced nations?
4. How can technology-driven processes build trust among victims, witnesses, and the global community?

Conclusion

These reflection questions invite readers to critically engage with the challenges and possibilities of international justice in a complex and interconnected world. By considering the delicate balance of sovereignty and accountability, the transformative role of civil society, and the ethical application of technology, readers can contribute to ongoing conversations about creating a more just and equitable global system.

Acknowledgments

This book is the culmination of collective effort, built upon the insights, expertise, and unwavering support of individuals and organizations dedicated to the pursuit of justice. Their contributions have enriched this work and given it depth, clarity, and purpose.

To the **researchers and collaborators**: I extend my deepest gratitude to those who devoted their time and intellect to this project. Your meticulous research and critical analysis were instrumental in shaping the narrative and ensuring its authenticity. This book stands as a reflection of your dedication to accuracy and truth.

To the **advocacy organizations**: A heartfelt acknowledgment goes to groups such as Amnesty International, Human Rights Watch, the International Criminal Court (ICC), and countless grassroots movements. Your tireless efforts to document atrocities, support victims, and demand accountability have been a source of profound inspiration. Your work reminds the world of the power of collective action and the enduring need for justice.

To the **technology innovators**: Thank you to the visionaries who are redefining the boundaries of justice through artificial intelligence, blockchain, and digital forensics. Your groundbreaking advancements have not only enhanced the tools available for accountability but also opened new possibilities for inclusion and transparency in global justice systems.

To the **survivors and advocates**: Above all, this book is for you. Your resilience in the face of unimaginable hardship and your determination to fight for justice are a testament to the strength of the human spirit. Your stories have been a guiding force in this work, a reminder of why the pursuit of justice must remain relentless and uncompromising.

This book is indebted to each of you. It is a shared endeavor, driven by the collective hope for a world where justice prevails and dignity is upheld for all. Thank you for your contributions, your courage, and your belief in the transformative power of accountability.

Sandeep Chavan

About the Series

Echoes of War: The Russia-Ukraine Conflict and Its Global Ripples by Sandeep Chavan

Exploring the profound impact of the Russia-Ukraine war across humanity, geopolitics, and beyond.

The Russia-Ukraine war, which began in 2022, has left an indelible mark on the world. It is a conflict that transcends borders, reshaping not just physical territories but also the political, economic, and environmental landscapes. *Echoes of War: The Russia-Ukraine Conflict and Its Global Ripples* is a compelling book series that examines the wide-reaching consequences of this historic conflict, offering nuanced insights into its various dimensions.

Titles within the Series

Humanitarian Impact

Shattered Lives: The Human Cost of the Russia-Ukraine War

Displacement, Resilience, and Hope Amid Conflict

A deep exploration of the human toll of war, focusing on displacement, refugee crises, and the enduring resilience of those affected.

Economic Effects

The War Economy: Global Disruptions from the Russia-Ukraine Crisis

How Conflict Redefined Trade, Energy, and Food Security

Analyzing the economic upheaval caused by the conflict, this book explores shifts in global trade, energy markets, and food security.

Geopolitical Shifts

Borders Redrawn: Global Politics in the Wake of the Russia-Ukraine War

NATO, Alliances, and the Changing Face of Power

A detailed look at how the war has reshaped alliances, redrawn geopolitical borders, and transformed global power dynamics.

Military Dynamics

Arms and Allies: Military Strategies of the Russia-Ukraine War

Tactics, Technology, and the Global Arms Race

This book dives into the military strategies, advanced technologies, and evolving alliances that have defined the conflict.

Environmental and Cyber Impacts

Collateral Damage: The Russia-Ukraine War's Toll on Earth and Cyberspace

Environmental Ruin and the Rise of Cyber Warfare

Exploring the hidden costs of war, this volume examines environmental devastation and the escalating role of cyber warfare.

Global Awareness and Legal Challenges

Justice in the Ashes: Accountability in the Russia-Ukraine War

War Crimes and the Pursuit of International Law

A compelling analysis of war crimes, international law, and the global pursuit of accountability and justice.

Discover the Series

Through comprehensive research, compelling narratives, and a global perspective, *Echoes of War* provides a definitive account of how the Russia-Ukraine conflict continues to reshape our world. Each book in the series examines a distinct aspect of the war's far-reaching consequences, offering readers a deeper understanding of its ripple effects across humanity, nations, and the planet.

Explore the *Echoes of War* series and join the conversation on one of the most defining conflicts of our time.

About the Author

Sandeep Chavan is an accomplished author, educator, and thinker with a deep interest in geopolitics, global economics, and their far-reaching impact on humanity. With decades of experience in industrial engineering and education, Chavan brings a unique blend of analytical rigor and empathetic understanding to his work. His writing is characterized by a keen ability to connect complex global phenomena with their real-world implications, making intricate subjects accessible to a wide audience.

In the *Echoes of War* series, Chavan explores the multidimensional impact of the Russia-Ukraine conflict on global politics, economies, societies, and ecosystems. Driven by an unrelenting curiosity to understand the ripple effects of war, he examines not just the immediate consequences but also the deeper, systemic changes that are reshaping the global order. His work reflects a commitment to uncovering truths, highlighting resilience, and fostering dialogue about the challenges and opportunities of an interconnected world.

Chavan's background in industrial engineering provides him with a systems-thinking approach, enabling him to analyze how geopolitical shifts and economic disruptions interconnect and cascade across sectors. His expertise is evident in his ability to dissect the complexities of international trade, energy markets, and technological advancements, and to contextualize these within the broader geopolitical framework.

As an author, Chavan is deeply committed to shedding light on the human cost of conflict while exploring pathways for resilience and recovery. His insights are informed by extensive research, global case studies, and a profound empathy for those whose lives are shaped by the forces of geopolitics. Through the *Echoes of War* series, Chavan not only documents the transformative impacts of the Russia-Ukraine war but also inspires readers to engage critically with the forces shaping our world today.

Chavan's work goes beyond analysis—it is a call to action, urging readers to consider their role in fostering a more equitable and sustainable global order. Whether examining humanitarian crises, economic disruptions, or the evolving dynamics of power, Chavan's voice is a guiding light in understanding the complexities of a world in flux.

Don't miss out!

Visit the website below and you can sign up to receive emails whenever SANDEEP CHAVAN publishes a new book. There's no charge and no obligation.

https://books2read.com/r/B-A-EPGPC-NAMLF

BOOKS 2 READ

Connecting independent readers to independent writers.

Did you love *Justice in the Ashes*? Then you should read *Win the Game You Didn't Choose*[1] by SANDEEP CHAVAN!

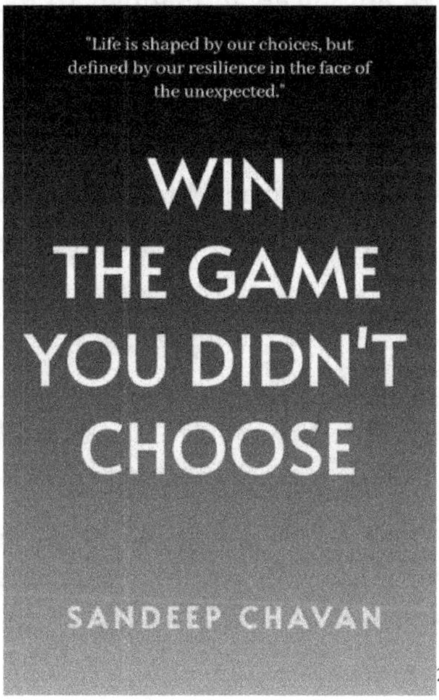

[2]

"Win The Game You Didn't Choose" by **Sandeep Chavan** is a powerful exploration of how to thrive amidst life's unexpected challenges, with a guiding philosophy that invites readers to find purpose and resilience in the uncharted terrains of their personal journeys. Chavan delves deeply into the ways life presents each of us with "games" we never asked for—situations that test our limits, reshape our values, and ultimately redefine what it means to "win."

In the early chapters, Chavan frames life's challenges as "unchosen games," those circumstances that are beyond our control yet deeply influence our lives. From health battles to career setbacks and family obligations, the book emphasizes that it's often the obstacles we never anticipated that reveal our true character. Through these experiences, readers are encouraged to recognize that success lies not in controlling every outcome but in understanding and accepting life's inherent unpredictability.

---

1. https://books2read.com/u/bPdXNA
2. https://books2read.com/u/bPdXNA

One of the book's central themes is the idea of "defining your own win." Chavan challenges conventional ideas of success and invites readers to craft personal definitions that resonate with their unique values, strengths, and aspirations. This approach empowers individuals to measure progress by their own standards, focusing on inner fulfillment rather than societal benchmarks.

Moving forward, Chavan provides a roadmap for self-discovery through understanding "game settings"—the individual circumstances, limitations, and choices that shape each person's journey. He highlights that by adjusting these settings, we gain the flexibility to influence our experiences, adapt our responses, and enhance our resilience. This adaptive mindset fosters a sense of agency, empowering readers to take charge of the aspects they can change while developing acceptance for those they cannot.

Chavan goes on to explore the twin forces of resilience and adaptability, showing how these traits work together to help us thrive amid life's inevitable changes. He emphasizes that resilience allows us to stand firm in the face of setbacks, while adaptability helps us to pivot and adjust our approach when circumstances shift. Together, they form the foundation for enduring growth and self-mastery.

Further, the book celebrates the power of small wins and personal progress, underscoring that even the smallest steps can have profound impacts on our journey. Chavan encourages readers to recognize the significance of incremental achievements, as these moments fuel the motivation needed to move forward. He reminds readers that personal growth often comes from celebrating the process itself, rather than waiting for a final destination.

The later chapters address the importance of learning from failure and crafting a legacy that reflects our authentic selves. Chavan invites readers to view setbacks not as failures but as essential learning experiences. By embracing these lessons, individuals can find new directions and create legacies built on resilience, courage, and integrity.

In *"Win The Game You Didn't Choose,"* Sandeep Chavan provides a thoughtful and practical guide for navigating life's uncertainties with grace and purpose. Through personal reflection, self-compassion, and intentional living, he offers readers the tools to find meaning, overcome adversity, and make the most of the game life presents them.

Read more at https://www.sandeepjchavan.com/.

Also by SANDEEP CHAVAN

Echoes of War: The Russia-Ukraine Conflict and Its Global Ripples

Shattered Lives

The War Economy

Borders Redrawn

Arms and Allies

Collateral Damage

Justice in the Ashes

Ultra Modern Life Philosophy

The Duality of Laughter and Tears

Compare to Accept

Standalone

It's Not AI, It's AHI - Amplified Human Intelligence

The Decision Paradox

The Four Sapiens

Malicious Script of Indian Polity

The IIT Legacy & Global Impact

The IIT Legacy & Global Impact

You are just a Version of Your Original

Win the Game You Didn't Choose

Always Keep Your Bags Packed

Reveal to Shield - Learn the Game of Facades
Engage Beyond Elections
Culture, Identity & Change: The Evolution of Indian Society
The Triangular Dynamics
Never Trust Without Doubt
If You Can't Change the Country, Leave the Country
Live Fearless with Fear
India: The Investment Magnet
Realignment
Powering a Billion Dreams
Universal Skill
Extension: From Brush to Algorithm

Watch for more at https://www.sandeepjchavan.com/.

www.ingramcontent.com/pod-product-compliance
Lightning Source LLC
LaVergne TN
LVHW052320200926
848481LV00002B/619

* 9 7 9 8 2 3 0 5 5 0 6 7 9 *